JBIOG
Khan
Kent, Zachary.

Genghis Khan /

RULERS OF THE MIDDLE AGES

GENGHIS KHAN

Invincible Ruler of the Mongol Empire

ZACHARY KENT

Enslow Publishers, Inc.
40 Industrial Road
Box 398
Berkeley Heights, NJ 07922
USA
http://www.enslow.com

Library of Congress Cataloging-in-Publication Data

Kent, Zachary.
    Genghis Khan : invincible ruler of the Mongol Empire / Zachary Kent.
        p. cm. — (Rulers of the middle ages)
    Includes bibliographical references and index.
    Audience: 11–12.
    ISBN-13: 978-0-7660-2715-2
    ISBN-10: 0-7660-2715-5
    1. Genghis Khan, 1162–1227—Juvenile literature. 2. Mongols—Kings and rulers—Biography—
    Juvenile literature. I. Title.
    DS22.K45 2007
    950'.21092—dc22
    [B]

                                     2006034062

Printed in the United States of America

10 9 8 7 6 5 4 3 2 1

To Our Readers:
We have done our best to make sure all Internet addresses in this book were active and appropriate
when we went to press. However, the author and the publisher have no control over and assume
no liability for the material available on those Internet sites or on other Web sites they may link
to. Any comments or suggestions can be sent by e-mail to comments@enslow.com or to the
address on the back cover.

Illustration Credits: AAAC/Topham/The Image Works, pp. 19, 58, 133; Bildarchiv Preussischer
Kulturbesitz/Art Resource, NY, p. 85; Enslow Publishers, Inc., pp. 10–11; Kharlamov Igor
Viktorovich/Shutterstock, p. 33; Nik Wheeler/Saudi Aramco World/PADIA, pp. 50, 137;
Original painting by Corey Wolfe, p. 4; Rémi Cauzid/Shutterstock, p. 16; Tan Kian
Khoon/Shutterstock, p. 78; Werner Forman/Art Resource, NY , pp. 99, 115.

Illustration Used in Design: Reproduced from *Full-Color Picture Sourcebook of Historic
Ornament*, published by Dover Publications, Inc.

Cover Illustration: Original painting by Corey Wolfe.

CONTENTS

ON THE SHORES OF LAKE BALJUNA

THE MONGOL CAVALRYMEN SPURRED THEIR tired horses forward. Mile after mile, the animals plodded ahead. Among the horsemen rode their leader, forty-one-year-old Genghis Khan. For many years, Genghis Khan had grown in power among the Mongol people. In the summer of 1203, however, his enemies had defeated him in battle. These enemies included members of the Kereit tribe and other warriors. Now, Genghis Khan and the remains of his beaten army were in retreat.

Genghis Khan and his horsemen rode to the far eastern edge of the Mongol country. When they reached the frontier of Manchuria, at last they stopped. North of the Onon River, they had come to Lake Baljuna. It was a large lake, surrounded by salty marshland.

THE OATH AT LAKE BALJUNA

Genghis Khan stepped down from the saddle of his horse. He gazed about and counted how many of his soldiers had remained with him. Only days before, he had commanded several thousand men. But only nineteen warriors had followed him all the way to Lake Baljuna.

There was only the muddy water of Lake Baljuna to drink. Genghis Khan and his warriors dipped their cups in the brown water. Genghis Khan swore an oath to his men. He thanked them for their loyalty and vowed never to forget it. Then he brought his cup to his lips and drank. All of his followers did the same. They promised to be forever loyal.

During the rest of the summer, Genghis Khan remained in camp. On the banks of Lake Baljuna, he and his men rested. They grazed their tired horses, letting them feed on the grass of the plains. Injured men nursed their wounds. Other warriors repaired broken weapons, sharpened the blades of knives and swords, and made arrows. Genghis Khan himself began making plans to attack his enemies. He sent messengers riding far and wide. It was their duty to carry word to his many scattered followers. Each day, more Mongols joined him at his camp. Genghis Khan also understood how to gain the help of other tribes. He had a great reputation as a fair and generous leader. His camp continued to grow in size.

Genghis Khan also sent spies into the enemy camps. The spies spread stories to make the enemy leaders suspicious of one another. This helped to weaken them. Some troops deserted the Kereit leader, Ong Khan, and returned to their homes. Some Kereit warriors even chose to join Genghis Khan.

The weather of autumn began to turn cool. Genghis Khan felt at last that his army was strong enough for action. He marched westward from the region of Lake Baljuna. His army headed toward the lands of Ong Khan.

DEFEATING THE KEREIT

While in camp, Genghis Khan had been joined by his brother Kasar. Kasar had left his family behind in the Kereit camp. Genghis Khan took advantage of this fact. He sent two of Kasar's servants ahead to Ong Khan. They were instructed to ask for permission to let Kasar return safely to his family. In truth, however, the two servants were spies. While in the Kereit camp, they looked to see if the Kereits were prepared for battle.

Ong Khan agreed to let Kasar return. The two servants who brought this news back to Genghis Khan gave their report. The army of Ong Khan was camped between the Kerulen and the Tula rivers. The Kereits were not prepared to fight a battle. Instead, they were eating and drinking at a huge feast. Genghis Khan acted quickly. With the two servants as guides, the Mongol horsemen made a secret march. They rushed toward the Kereit camp at Jejerundur. Wisely, Genghis Khan had sent men ahead with extra horses along the route. Tired horses were replaced with fresh ones, as needed. Genghis Khan's army hurried forward without rest for an entire day and night.

At last, they reached the Kereit camp. Suddenly, the Mongol horsemen galloped among the enemy. This was the moment and the place that would decide Genghis

Khan's future. If he lost now, all of his support would disappear. The battle raged for three days and three nights. Every time the Kereits tried to break out of their camp, the fierce Mongols forced them back. To avoid certain death, many Kereits surrendered. Ong Khan and his son Senggum at last saved themselves by escaping across the grassy plains. In the end, the Kereit army was broken and scattered. Ong Khan was killed by a Naiman who did not recognize him, and Senggum was later captured and killed.

In a single battle, Genghis Khan had regained all of his lost Mongol territory. He also had completely conquered the Kereits and taken their lands as well. In addition, he fulfilled the vow he had made at Lake Baljuna. He would continue to spread his power in the next years and reward his loyal followers.

Genghis Khan's children and grandchildren would live to see a Mongol Empire that stretched from the Pacific Ocean all the way to the Mediterranean Sea. It would cover territory from Siberia in the north to the Himalayan Mountains in the south. During his own lifetime, Genghis Khan would conquer more lands and people than the Romans did in four hundred years. He would become the leader of more people than anyone in history. The Mongol Empire would cover more than 11 million square miles, more land than the entire continent of North America. Yet Genghis Khan had begun life very humbly, with hardly a place to call his home.

THE MONGOL BOYHOOD OF TEMUJIN

IN THE MID-1200s, A BOOK CALLED *THE SECRET History of the Mongols* was written. It is often referred to as *The Secret History*. This book told the life story of the Mongol leader Genghis Khan. Some historians believe the book was written by the Mongol chief judge Shigi Khutukhu.[1] It is uncertain if the contents—containing myth, legend, and history—of this biography are completely true. However, much of what is known today about the boyhood of Genghis Khan is learned from *The Secret History*.

THE LAND OF THE MONGOLS

A great mountain called Burkhan Khaldun stands in northeast Asia. The cool waters of two rivers, the Onon and the Kerulen, flow down from this mountain. Between these two rivers is found the homeland of the Mongols.

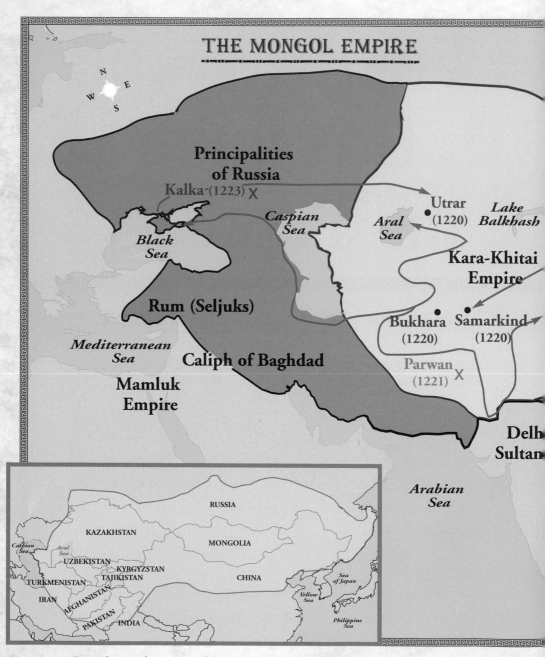

THE MONGOL EMPIRE

Principalities of Russia

Kalka (1223) X

Caspian Sea

Utrar (1220)

Lake Balkhash

Aral Sea

Kara-Khitai Empire

Black Sea

Rum (Seljuks)

Bukhara (1220)

Samarkind (1220)

Mediterranean Sea

Caliph of Baghdad

Parwan (1221) X

Mamluk Empire

Delh Sultan

Arabian Sea

RUSSIA

KAZAKHSTAN

MONGOLIA

Caspian Sea

Aral Sea

UZBEKISTAN

KYRGYZSTAN

TAJIKISTAN

TURKMENISTAN

CHINA

Sea of Japan

IRAN

AFGHANISTAN

Yellow Sea

PAKISTAN

INDIA

Philippine Sea

Genghis Khan would unite the Mongol clans into a single, mighty empire. He conquered territory that covers many present-day countries (inset). Later, under Kublai Khan, the Mongol Empire stretched even into Europe at its height.

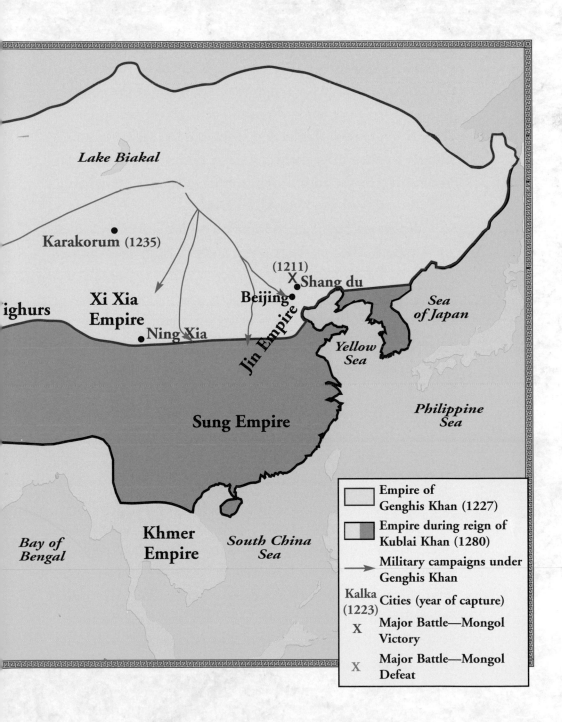

Lake Biakal

Karakorum (1235)

Xi Xia
Empire

ighurs

Ning Xia

(1211)
X Shang du
Beijing

Jin Empire

Sea
of Japan

Yellow
Sea

Sung Empire

Philippine
Sea

Bay of
Bengal

Khmer
Empire

South China
Sea

	Empire of Genghis Khan (1227)
	Empire during reign of Kublai Khan (1280)
→	Military campaigns under Genghis Khan
Kalka (1223)	Cities (year of capture)
X	Major Battle—Mongol Victory
X	Major Battle—Mongol Defeat

This high mountain, Burkhan Khaldun, would play an important role in the life of Genghis Khan. Present-day Mongolia is located on a high plateau. Most of the country stands more than three thousand feet above sea level. To the east and west, the land is bordered by high mountain ranges. In the north stand the great mountains and forests of Siberia. To the south lie mountains, forests, grasslands, and the sands of the huge Gobi Desert.

The grassy plains of Mongolia's high plateau are called the steppes. The weather on the steppes is harsh. The sun bakes the land in the summer. Icy winds blow across the frozen ground in the winter. The people who lived in the region became tough because of their environment. Living on the steppes had always been very difficult.

In eastern Mongolia, during the 1100s, a nation grew. It became known by the name Mongol. The Chinese sometimes pronounced the name "Menggu." The ancient Chinese historian Li Xinchuan wrote, "The Menggu . . . people are strong and warlike . . ."[2]

The Mongols grouped themselves together into clans. A clan is a group of people related by common ancestors. This means they were related by blood, or as the Mongols called it by the "bones."[3] For a time, Kabul Khan of the Borjigin clan of Mongols united the people of the steppes. The Mongols, however, were surrounded by more powerful tribes. These tribes included the Kereit and the Naiman in the west and south. The Merkit tribe occupied lands to the north, and the great tribe called the Tatars lived in the east. During the 1160s, Tatar warriors attacked the Mongols. The Tatars sent the Mongol clans fleeing in all directions. The medieval Persian historian Juvaini later wrote of the Mongols, "They had neither ruler nor leader. The tribes lived apart . . . they were not united . . ."[4]

The Mongols separated into their small clans. Each clan had to struggle to survive. Often they fought with one another. The Mongol religious leader Teb Tengri later declared, "Everyone was feuding. Rather than sleep they robbed each other . . . The whole nation was in rebellion. Rather than rest they fought each other."[5]

MONGOL LIFE

In the 1160s, two Mongol clans shared the grassy region between the Onon and the Kerulen rivers. These were the Borjigin and the Taijiut clans. The Mongol clans never stayed in one place very long. There is an ancient history book written by members of the Khitan people of Asia. It describes the roaming Mongols: "They have no agriculture, hunting is their primary occupation; they . . . migrate, following the seasonal supplies of water and pasture . . ."[6]

Many Mongols kept herds of horses, cows, goats, camels, and yaks, as well as flocks of sheep. Almost all Mongols had horses and sheep. These Mongols moved several times each year, in search of grassy pastures. They lived on the higher steppes in the summer. Each autumn, they traveled to the lowlands, as the weather turned cold.

Religion played a large part in the lives of the Mongols. They called their god "Mongke Koke Tengri" (Eternal Blue Heaven). The Mongols sometimes climbed to the

MONGOL HERDS

Mongol methods of herding have changed little since the 1200s. Even today, sheep are an important part of Mongol life. Sheep and goats are often herded together. Goats have a natural skill for finding good grass upon which herds can graze. A single shepherd can watch a herd of as many as one thousand sheep and goats. Trained dogs keep wild animals, such as wolves, away from the herds.

Sheep provide the Mongols with meat (mutton) to eat. Sheepskins can be sewed into warm winter coats. Sheep wool is pressed into felt, which is used to make the walls of Mongol yurts.

tops of mountains. In this way, they believed they could become closer to Tengri. While praying to Tengri, they respectfully removed their hats. They also took off their belts and lay them around their shoulders. The Mongols believed that springs of water had godly powers. No one was allowed to make flowing water dirty. As a result, the Mongols did not often wash themselves, their clothes, or their cooking pots. In addition to Heaven, the Mongols worshiped the earth, the sun, and the moon. They believed local spirits could be found on the mountain peaks, on the land, and in the water. These spirits deserved deep respect. The Mongols also prayed to the spirits of the dead.

HOMES ON WHEELS

The Mongols lived in round tents, called yurts. The roof and walls of each yurt were made of a type of pressed wool called felt. The felt walls of each yurt were supported by a wooden frame made of willow wood. Small yurts were most practical, because they were easy to heat in winter. There was a small hole in the roof through which fireplace smoke could pour out. The yurt fireplace was used for heat and cooking. The entrance to each yurt always faced south. Whenever Mongols looked out their doorways, they could see the sun in the sky, which they worshiped.

When the Mongols traveled, they took apart their smaller yurts. They rolled up the felt roofs and walls and lifted the rolls onto wagons. Larger tents were lifted complete onto oxcarts. These great carts sometimes measured twenty feet wide (six meters). The wooden wheels of the great carts were taller than a man. It took the strength of eleven pairs of oxen to pull one.

MONGOL FOODS

The Mongols depended on their animal herds for a good part of their diets. They milked their sheep, goats, and cows. They drank the fresh milk and made cheeses, yogurt,

MEASURING TIME

The Mongols measured time in twelve-year cycles. Each year was represented by the name of an animal. The names of the Mongol years during each twelve-year cycle were: Rat, Ox, Tiger, Hare, Dragon, Snake, Horse, Sheep, Monkey, Hen, Dog, and Pig.[7] This is very much like the zodiac that is used by the Chinese today.

and curds from it. They also made an alcoholic drink from mare's milk. It was called *kumiss*. To make kumiss, they beat the mares' milk in large leather bags that hung from wooden frames. The solid, sour curds in the milk separated from the liquid whey. By a natural chemical process called fermentation, the whey turned into alcohol.

Meat supplied an additional part of their diet. The long, cold winter was the season for hunting. The young animals that had been born in the spring had grown large enough to hunt by winter. Mongol men hunted rabbits, wolves, elk, wild sheep, and wild boars across the steppes and in the northern forests. They trained hawks and falcons to capture smaller animals. At meals, Mongol

These yurts are still used today in China and Mongolia. This is the type of home that the Mongols of the Middle Ages lived in.

families always ate from a common pot. Different kinds of meat often filled the pot.

KIDNAPPING A WIFE

In the 1160s, a warrior named Yesugei was one of the leaders of the Borjigin clan of Mongols. One winter day, Yesugei was out hunting with two of his brothers. In the distance, they noticed a man on horseback. The man was riding beside a cart on which sat a young woman. The man was a Merkit warrior named Chiledu. The young woman was his new wife, Hoelun, of the Onggirat clan of Mongols. It was common practice on the steppes for warriors to steal the women of rival tribes. Yesugei decided he would kidnap Hoelun and take her for his own wife.

Yesugei and his brothers spurred their horses and charged after Chiledu and Hoelun. Chiledu galloped away, hoping the three Mongols would chase after him and leave his wife alone. Yesugei and his brothers did chase after Chiledu for a while. But at last they gave up. They rode back to where Hoelun had been left. Yesugei guided Hoelun's cart back to his camp. He made Hoelun his new wife.

THE BIRTH OF TEMUJIN

Yesugei's clan was camped beside the Onon River. In time, Hoelun gave birth to their first son. When the baby was born, a thick lump of blood was discovered clutched in one

17

of his hands. The superstitious people of the clan could not decide what the blood clot meant.

When the baby was born, Yesugei had just returned from a war against the Tatar tribe to the east. During his battles, he had captured a Tatar chief named Temujin. As a reminder of this event, it was said Yesugei gave his baby son the same name as the captured chief.[8] The boy was to be called Temujin.

There is a second possible reason how Temujin got his name. The Mongol word for blacksmith is "Temerchi." It is thought by some scholars that Yesugei's family were blacksmiths, the makers of horseshoes and other iron items. These scholars believe that Temujin got his name from the word "Temerchi."[9] No matter how Temujin got his name, no one could guess that he would one day grow up to become the great Mongol ruler Genghis Khan.

Different dates have been given for Temujin's birth. The most common date, however, is the year 1162.[10] As the years passed, Hoelun and Yesugei had three more sons together. They were Kasar, Kachun, and Temuge. Their final child was a daughter named Temulin. Mongol men were permitted to have more than one wife. Yesugei had another wife, in addition to Hoelun. Her name was Sochigel. With Sochigel, Yesugei had two more sons named Belgutei and Begter.

A MONGOL CHILDHOOD

Temujin spent much of his childhood near the Onon River. Yesugei's Borjigin clan often camped beside that

A stone slab with the image of Genghis Khan marks what is thought to be his birthplace, at Dadal Sum, Mongolia, near the Onon River.

river. All Mongol children learned to ride horseback while very young. At about the age of three, Hoelun tied Temujin onto the back of a horse for his first riding lesson.[11] When he was about four or five, Temujin was given a small bow and some arrows. His parents encouraged him to learn how to hunt on horseback. The boy rode through the woods and across the steppes, shooting at birds. In wintertime, Temujin often glided on the ice of the Onon River with his brothers and sister and other children. They wore skates made from animal bones.

One of Temujin's childhood friends was a boy who was a little bit older. His name was Jamuka. Jamuka was a member of the Jadaran clan of Mongols. Jamuka's family often camped near Temujin's beside the riverbank. The two boys spent much time together in camp and hunting in the woods. As the two boys grew older, they decided to become "andas." Andas were blood brothers. Andas were often considered closer than birth brothers. Andas, after all, had chosen one another. In formal anda ceremonies, Temujin and Jamuka exchanged animal knucklebones. New Mongol andas also traditionally drank a few drops of their own blood mixed in a cup.

FINDING A WIFE

When Temujin was about nine years old, Yesugei decided it was time to find his son a wife. Mongols married at an early age. It was a way for different clans and tribes to form important alliances. With a marriage connection, people agreed to support and protect one another. Yesugei planned to find his son a wife among the Olkunut. The Olkunut were a clan of the Onggirat Mongols. It was the clan of Hoelun's family.

Father and son set out on horseback for the long trip to the Olkunut camp. During their journey, however, they came upon another camp. It belonged to the Onggirat tribe that lived in the rich pastures to the east of the Gobi Desert. Yesugei and Temujin rode into the camp and were welcomed by the chieftain, Dei Sechen. When Dei Sechen saw nine-year-old Temujin for the first time, he was impressed by his appearance. According to *The Secret History*, Dei Sechen told Yesugei, "Your son has flashing eyes and a lively face."[12]

Dei Sechen's daughter, Borte, was a little bit older than Temujin. The two children played together in camp and seemed to like each other. Yesugei and Dei Sechen agreed Temujin and Borte should marry one day. Dei Sechen insisted, however, that Temujin must live with the chieftain's own family until the marriage day arrived. "Leave him here with me," Dei Sechen told Yesugei, "to become my son-in-law."[13]

THE DEATH OF YESUGEI

Yesugei left Temujin to live with Dei Sechen's clan of the Onggirat tribe. He believed the marriage of Temujin and Borte would help form a valuable alliance between clans. He began the long ride back to his own Borjigin clan. During the journey, Yesugei had to travel through Tatar territory. The Tatars were longtime enemies of the Mongols. As a warrior, Yesugei had fought them often.

One evening, Yesugei happened upon a Tatar camp. It was common courtesy on the steppes to invite a traveler to eat. Yesugei stopped and sat in the firelight with the Tatars. He hoped none of them would recognize him. Some of these Tatars, however, did recognize Yesugei. They secretly mixed some poison into the food that he was given to eat.

After his meal, Yesugei left the Tatar camp and continued on his journey home. By the time he reached his own camp, the effects of the poison had made him very sick. From his bed of felt blankets, Yesugei called for Monglik. Monglik was one of his loyal followers. Yesugei asked Monglik to ride and bring Temujin back to him. Yesugei knew his end was near. He wanted to see his son one last time. Monglik hurried and fetched Temujin home. Sadly, though, by the time Temujin reached his father's side, his father had died.

DAYS OF HUNGER

Yesugei left behind two wives and seven young children. At the time of his death, the Borjigin clan was camped beside the Onon River. Members of the Taijiut clan were camped with them. Yesugei had been the leader of the entire camp. As a respected warrior, he had helped protect these people. As a skilled hunter, he had helped fill the camp pots with food. After his death, though, the Taijiuts decided they did not want to support Yesugei's two widows and his seven children. The death of Yesugei had opened up the chance for a new leader to take control of the entire camp. The leader of the Taijiut clan, Targutai, decided to grab the opportunity. Targutai rose up and claimed leadership of the Yesugei's Borjigin clan as well. To avoid future claims of leadership by Yesugei's children, Targutai chose to desert Hoelun and her family. He would shut them out of their clan altogether. Within days of Yesugei's death, Targutai rode off with all who would follow him.

Hoelun soon discovered herself alone on the steppes. Remaining with her were just a few old servants, her children, and Yesugei's second wife and two sons. She bravely took up the daily work of providing them with food. She filled her basket with wild plants that could be eaten as salad. She dug up soft roots along the river, as well as wild onions. In autumn, she gathered wild apples and bird cherries. She probably picked pine seeds and the seeds of the apricot bush, which is found in Mongolia. Hoelun struggled to find food any way she could.

Young Temujin and his brothers did their best to help. They made wooden arrows, with sharpened bones attached for points. With bows and arrows, they hunted mice and other small animals on the steppes. They also made fishhooks out of bent bone needles. With these, they sat on the Onon riverbank fishing. Whatever small fish they caught went into the family cook pot. The family survived, and Hoelun's children grew up strong and healthy.

The Murder of Begter

Temujin's relationship with his half brothers, Begter and Belgutei, was not a happy one. Begter was the oldest son of Yesugei. It seemed Begter wanted to be accepted as the new head of the family. Temujin was the oldest of Hoelun's children, however. Temujin wished to take his father's place at the head of the Borjigin clan. As time passed, Temujin and Kasar often argued with Begter and Belgutei. One day, Temujin told his mother that he and Kasar had shot a bird with an arrow. But Begter and Belgutei had taken it from them. On another day, Temujin and Kasar complained that they had caught a fish, but Begter and Belgutei had stolen that, too. Hoelun tried to keep peace among the brothers. According to *The Secret History*, she reminded her sons, "Apart from our own shadow we have no friends."[14]

In the end, however, to show that he was head of the family, Temujin decided to do a terrible thing. He decided he would murder Begter. He got his brother Kasar to join in his plan. One day, they found Begter sitting on a grassy hill near camp, looking after the grazing horses. Temujin and Kasar silently crept toward him through the high grass. They snuck up on Begter and finally reached easy striking distance. Then the boys suddenly stood and revealed themselves. Already they had arrows on their bows, drawn and pointed at Begter. Begter made no attempt to escape. He refused to show fear. He only folded his arms and asked that Temujin spare the life of his brother Belgutei.

24

In another moment, Temujin let go his arrow. It hit Begter in the chest. At nearly the same time, Kasar let his own arrow fly. It struck Begter in the back. After killing Begter, Temujin and Kasar returned to their yurt. Before they could speak, Hoelun saw the ashamed looks on their faces. She knew that they had done an awful thing. It is written in *The Secret History* that she cried out, "You murderers!"[15] The killing of Begter, however, finally brought peace to Hoelun's camp. From that day forward, everyone accepted teenage Temujin as head of the family.

THE YOUNG CHIEFTAIN

WHEN HE MURDERED HIS HALF BROTHER Begter, Temujin was about fourteen or fifteen years old.[1] The murder was regarded among the Mongols as a horrible act. Although Temujin had become head of his family, he had also become a renegade. He had gone against Mongol custom. If caught, he would be punished for his crime. The Taijiut and Borjigin clans claimed the territory located between the Onon and Kerulen rivers. Temujin still boldly grazed his family's horses in that place. To capture Temujin, the chieftain Targutai decided to swoop down and raid Hoelun's camp with his Taijiut warriors. Temujin's capture would bring his family and the entire Borjigin clan more completely under Targutai's control.

A TAIJIUT PRISONER

Raiding Taijiut warriors galloped into Hoelun's camp. Surprised, Temujin jumped on a horse and escaped into the woods. The Taijiuts chased him, and at last surrounded the thicket where Temujin hid. For nine days, Temujin refused to surrender. At last, however, tired and hungry, Temujin was captured.

The Taijiuts brought Temujin back to their camp. They treated him as a prisoner. They fastened a great wooden collar on his shoulders. His wrists were tied to the ends of the collar. This forced him to keep his arms outstretched from side to side. This collar was called a "cangue." It was heavy and rubbed his skin raw. The cangue prevented Temujin from lying flat. He could never sleep comfortably. In this condition, Temujin remained a prisoner of the Taijiuts. Each night, he was kept in a different yurt in the Taijiut camp. In this way, the work of keeping him prisoner was shared by the entire camp.

Escape From the Taijiuts

In the summers, the Taijiuts celebrated the Day of the Red Moon. In the Taijiut camp, there was much feasting and drinking on that holiday. That evening, Temujin found himself guarded by only one weak boy. Everyone else was celebrating. Determined to be free, Temujin suddenly swung his shoulders. The cangue struck the young guard on the head and knocked him unconscious. Temujin ran to the Onon riverbank and waded into the water. He hid there with only his face above the surface, so he could breathe.

When they learned of his escape, the Taijiuts sent out search parties. It was a man named Sorqan-Shira who noticed Temujin in the water. Sorqan-Shira was a member of the Suldus clan. He and his family were living among the Taijiuts as servants. One night, while a prisoner, Temujin had slept in Sorqan-Shira's yurt. Sorqan-Shira's family had treated him kindly. Now, Sorqan-Shira crouched beside the water and whispered to Temujin. According to *The Secret History*, he told Temujin that the Taijiuts were jealous of Temujin and fearful of his clever mind. "Just lie where you are," he warned him. "I will not give you away."[2]

That night, when all was quiet, Temujin climbed out of the water. Carefully, he crept to Sorqan-Shira's yurt. When he thought it was safe, he entered the yurt and asked Sorqan-Shira's family for help. It was dangerous for these Suldus servants to help a runaway prisoner. But they removed the cangue and burned it. Then they hid Temujin in a cart filled with wool. The next day, the Taijiuts continued their hunt for Temujin. But he remained safely hidden under the pile of wool. When it was dark, Sorqan-Shira gave Temujin a horse. After the moon went down, Temujin rode out of the camp. In time, he rejoined his mother and his family. He had survived his time among the Taijiuts, and with luck and daring he had escaped.

Stolen Horses

Temujin and his family made camp at the foot of the great mountain, Burkhan Khaldun. One day, a gang of robbers raided their camp. The robbers stole eight of the family's nine horses. The family's only other horse was not in the camp at the time. Belgutei had been out hunting on it. When Belgutei returned, Temujin mounted the horse. He vowed he would ride after the robbers and recover the stolen horses.

For three days, Temujin followed the horse tracks across the steppes. On the fourth day, he met thirteen-year-old Bo'orchu who was a member of the Arulat clan of Mongols. Temujin described the purpose of his journey. When Temujin finished his story, Bo'orchu volunteered to help him. The two teenagers rode off together.

It was another three days before they caught up with the horse thieves. In the dark of night, Temujin and Bo'orchu quietly rode forward. Suddenly, they galloped into the robber camp. They found the stolen horses, and quickly galloped away again. The robbers chased after them. Temujin turned in his saddle and shot an arrow at them. His fierceness frightened some of the robbers, who gave up the chase. The two boys successfully escaped in the nighttime darkness with all of the horses.

Temujin wished to reward Bo'orchu for his help. "Friend, would I ever have found my horses without you?" he said. "Let us share them. How many do you wish?" Bo'orchu refused to take any. "I joined you," he responded, "because I saw that you were in trouble and in need of help."[3]

Bo'orchu's father was proud of his son's actions and of his friendship with the fierce Temujin. He told Bo'orchu to remain with the young Mongol leader. When Temujin returned to his camp, Bo'orchu came with him. Bo'orchu

ANOTHER ADVENTURE

Young Temujin surely had other adventures. The medieval Persian historian Rashid al-Din wrote down Temujin's telling of one story: "I was riding alone on one occasion. Six men lay in ambush along the route . . . As I approached them I drew my sword and attacked. They [shot] arrows at me but these all flew past without one hitting me. I hacked the men down and rode on . . . On my return I passed close to their bodies."[4] Temujin claimed that as a result of this adventure he herded the six horses of the men home.

became the first follower of Temujin who was not a member of his family.

THE SABLE CLOAK

In 1178, Temujin turned sixteen. He had not seen his promised wife, Borte, since his father's death seven years before. Temujin decided it was time Borte should be brought to live with him. As a result, he rode the long distance to the Onggirat camp to claim her. With his half brother Belgutei, he journeyed along the Kerulen River. At last, they found the Onggirat camp and the yurt belonging to Dei Sechen.

Dei Sechen was happy to welcome the young man who was promised to become his son-in-law. Borte had not married, but was still waiting for Temujin. Together, Temujin, Belgutei, and Borte set off toward home. Borte brought a wedding gift with her. It was a beautiful cloak, a long cape, made from the fur of sables. The sable is a mammal found throughout northern Europe and northern Asia. It looks somewhat like a mink, and its glossy black fur is greatly valued.

Temujin desired to become the leader of the Borjigin clan. He decided to use the sable cloak to help him get what he wanted. To the west, at the headwaters of the Tula River, lay the land of the great Kereit tribe. Temujin, together with his brothers Kasar and Belgutei, rode to the Kereit camp. They looked for Toghrul, the leader of the Kereits. Years earlier, Yesugei had joined Toghrul in the war that had established Toghrul as ruler of the Kereit people.

When Temujin found Toghrul, he sat with him. "In earlier days," Temujin reminded him, "you swore friendship with my father, Yesugei." With these words, Temujin handed Toghrul the black sable cloak. Toghrul gladly accepted the valuable gift. The two agreed to form an alliance and to help each other. According to *The Secret History*, Toghrul told Temujin, "I will reunite your scattered people."[5]

THE KIDNAPPING OF BORTE

Temujin and his brothers rode back to their family camp beside the Kerulen River. It was lucky for Temujin that he had made his alliance with Toghrul when he did. He was very soon in need of Toghrul's help. Not long after he had returned home, three hundred Merkit warriors raided his camp.

Early one morning as the family slept in their yurt, the Merkits galloped into the camp. Temujin, his brothers, and a few followers sprang up and fled. It was all that they could do to escape capture. But while Temujin and his brothers successfully escaped, Borte and Sochigel, who was Belgutei's mother, were caught and taken away.

Temujin climbed to the top of the sacred mountain Bhurkan Khaldun. There, he gave thanks to the Eternal Blue Heaven for his escape from the Merkits. According to *The Secret History*, he declared, "For the second time Mount Bhurkan-Khaldun has saved my poor life."[6] For three days, Temujin prayed on the mountain top. In the end, he decided he must fight in order to get Borte back. He came down from the mountain and journeyed to Toghrul's camp. He told Toghrul what had happened. He asked Toghrul to join him on a raid against the Merkits.

Toghrul was a longtime enemy of the Merkits. He promised Temujin, "In gratitude for the black sable cloak we will rescue your wife Borte, even if we have to massacre every Merkit!"[7] He gave Temujin instructions, so that they could prepare for battle. Temujin was to send a messenger to his anda Jamuka. Over the years, Jamuka had made himself chief of the Jadaran clan of Mongols. Temujin's messenger asked that Jamuka join in the attack. Like Temujin, Jamuka had become an ally of Toghrul.

DEFEAT OF THE MERKIT

Toghrul and Jamuka both had many followers willing to ride into battle. Temujin, however, had only a few followers. Now he had to raise his first army. A Mongol army consisted of warriors who gathered under a leader to fight a military campaign. During a campaign, they would attack their enemies in the hope of capturing their riches and enslaving their people. Afterward, the warriors would split up and return home with their prizes. Temujin's growing reputation as a daring and fearless warrior helped him gather an army now. As the word went out across the steppes, Mongols left their flocks, mounted their horses, and rode to Temujin's camp.

The armies of Toghrul and Jamuka gathered with Temujin's small force at the headwaters of the Onon River. The headwaters are the source of a river. It is the place where the water first flows down from mountain springs

This part of the Altay Mountains in Russia was once part of the Mongol Empire.

and melted snow. Together, the united army rode to the Kereit camp. The camp was located between the Tula and the Orkhon rivers. When the moment at last arrived, the warriors galloped forward, shooting their arrows.

The Merkit were swiftly defeated. Merkit survivors of the fight fearfully retreated downstream. The attackers rode among the Merkit yurts, taking loot wherever they found it. Temujin galloped about, calling Borte's name. At last, Borte heard his voice and rushed to him. Loving husband and wife were finally reunited. According to *The Secret History*, Temujin joyfully exclaimed, "I have found [Borte whom] I was looking for."[8]

The attack on the Merkit camp was a complete success. The Merkit women, the Merkit cattle, and the contents of the Merkit yurts were all divided among the raiders. The success of the raid greatly increased Temujin's fame as a leader. Before the raid against the Merkit, Temujin had called himself a chief. However, he did not have many followers. He did not have any real power. After the raid, though, he had both followers and growing power with which to lead them. Temujin had a camp he could rule with pride and an army he could train.

While she was a prisoner, Borte had been forced to become the wife of a Merkit warrior named Chilger. Months after Borte's rescue, Temujin learned that she was pregnant. Her first son was born in 1179. Temujin did not know if he or Chilger was the father. Temujin named the boy Jochi, which means "visitor" or "guest" in the Mongol language. Temujin always accepted Jochi as his own son.[9]

In the years that followed, Temujin and Borte would have three other sons, named Chagatai, Ogodei, and Tolui.

THE END OF A FRIENDSHIP

After destroying the Merkit camp, Temujin and Jamuka decided to travel and camp together. They renewed their relationship as anda. They ate their meals together and in the evenings drank together. At night, they slept side by side, sharing the same blanket. During the next year and a half, Temujin and Jamuka were as close as two friends could be.

Their friendly relationship could not last. Both men were full of ambition. Both wished to become the leader of all the Mongols. Temujin desired more followers so that he could increase his power. In May 1181, Jamuka ordered his people to break spring camp. The two men and their followers would journey toward greener summer pastures. Temujin and Jamuka rode together at the head of the long line of moving carts, wagons, and herds of animals.

Borte knew of her husband's ambition. At the end of one day's journey, she told Temujin, "We must not stop; we must march on through the night, it is better to be parted from him."[10] So, while Jamuka and his Jadaran followers halted, Temujin's people kept moving ahead. Slowly, the two clans divided and went their separate ways. The next time Temujin and Jamuka would meet, they would be hated enemies.

KHAN OF THE MONGOLS

<hr />

THE DEFEAT OF THE MERKITS HAD MADE Temujin a hero to many of the Mongol people. More and more, Mongols looked to Temujin to unite all of the separate Mongol clans. One Mongol shaman claimed that God had told him "I have given the whole surface of the earth to Temujin and to his sons."[1]

In the summer of 1189, twenty-seven-year-old Temujin called together a meeting of many of the Mongol leaders. Such a meeting was called a *kuriltai* in the language of the Mongols. Thousands of Mongols gathered for the kuriltai. They set up their yurts beside Temujin's camp.

TEMUJIN BECOMES GENGHIS KHAN

The Mongols called their leaders *khans*. Temujin had called for this kuriltai so that a new khan could be elected. He wished to be that person.

The chief Mongols at the kuriltai recognized Temujin's skills as a leader. They gathered before him and sang a song. "We will make you Khan," they sang. "You shall ride at our head, against our enemies. We will fling ourselves like the lightning upon your foes . . . If we disobey you on the day of battle, take our flocks from us, our wives and children, throw our worthless heads out on the steppe . . ."[2] After singing these words, they elected Temujin their khan. He was given the title Chinggis Khan, which is thought to mean "Lord of the Earth."[3] This name became better known through a later Arab spelling as Genghis Khan.

The decision to make Temujin their leader was celebrated by the gathered Mongols with a great feast. The Kereit leader Toghrul was pleased to learn of the election. "It is right and proper that you have elected my son Temujin as your leader," he stated. "How could you Mongols be without a leader? Do not go back on your decision."[4]

Temujin, now Genghis Khan, had made his claim to be ruler of all of the Mongols. Immediately, he decided to reorganize his camp. He put his most faithful followers into two groups as his bodyguard. They became his Quiver Bearers and his Sword Bearers. Among other duties, these followers were responsible for preparing food and drink in the camp. Other followers were to take care of the horses. Still others were given jobs keeping wagons and carts repaired.

Genghis Khan assigned these positions, and others, according to the ability and loyalty of each warrior. It did not matter to him if they were of noble blood or of humble birth. All of his life, Genghis Khan would give his followers and soldiers equal chances to prove their worth. Now, he gave his first two followers, Bo'orchu and a young man named Jelme, the important positions of personal assistants. Altogether, he would keep one hundred fifty warriors on duty at all hours to keep his camp safe. There would be seventy day guards and eighty night guards. This bodyguard was called the Keshig.[5]

Genghis Khan was always on the lookout for ways to strengthen his position as leader. He realized he had much to do in order to become a success. Although he had become a Mongol khan, he was a small khan. He claimed as his territory the traditional Mongol lands located between the Onon and the Kerulen rivers. But there were other Mongol clan leaders who made the same claim. To make his tribe stronger, Genghis Khan concentrated on training his warriors. Day after day, his horsemen rode back and forth in battle formations across the steppes. They practiced charges and retreats, shooting arrows as they did so. They learned how to follow orders without question. Genghis Khan was determined to make his army the best possible.

A GROWING REPUTATION

Genghis Khan had picked an important moment to claim Mongol leadership. There were many small clans all over the steppes. They realized they needed a strong leader in order to survive. Many clans recognized that Genghis Khan might be that leader. As the months passed, Mongol people joined Genghis Khan in growing numbers. People of the Besut, Suldus, Jalair, and other clans all rode into his camp.

The people who joined Genghis Khan believed he would provide them with a better life. It was known that Genghis Khan treated his own followers with kindness. He gave his people gifts of horses and furs. The *Yuanshi*, a Chinese book, declared that Genghis Khan "dresses his people in his own clothes, he permits them to ride his own horses; this man could certainly bring peace to the tribe and rule the nation."[6] As Genghis Khan's reputation grew, so did his following.

A Mongol Rival

In 1190, only one year after Genghis Khan's election, he was forced to go to war. Jamuka, his childhood friend and *anda*, was leader of the Jadaran clan. Jamuka was ambitious, too. He had been gathering Mongol followers and had declared himself the rightful Mongol khan. Genghis Khan and Jamuka had become rivals.

Sometime earlier, one of Genghis Khan's followers had killed one of Jamuka's relatives. The two men had argued over a stolen horse. Jamuka used the murder as an excuse to start a war. Jamuka marched out to battle Genghis Khan. Jamuka had gathered warriors from his own Jadaran clan as well as from thirteen other clans. Messengers brought Genghis Khan news of the enemy advance. He rode out with his own warriors to meet them. The two sides battled at a place called Dalan Baljut.

Genghis Khan's soldiers were defeated, and many of his men fled the field. Genghis Khan retreated to the headwaters of the Onon River. The loyalty of his men saved him from complete disaster. Stories of cruelty did not help Jamuka win new followers. It was said that after the battle, he had seventy prisoners boiled alive in large pots. Another story told how he had cut off the head of a captured officer and tied it to his horse's tail. The bloody head dangled behind his horse as he rode along. Some of Jamuka's own soldiers deserted their harsh leader and joined Genghis Khan's camp.

The fight at Dalan Baljut proved a turning point for Genghis Khan. He had lost the battle, but he had won even greater support among the Mongol people. Many Mongols decided they preferred Genghis Khan to Jamuka in the struggle for leadership.

A RAID ON THE TATARS

Jamuka's victory at Dalan Baljut caused a crisis in Mongolia. Genghis Khan's defeat had weakened his alliance with the Kereit leader Toghrul. As a result, in 1192, Toghrul's brother Erke Kara seized the chance to drive Toghrul from his country. Genghis Khan gave Toghrul shelter in his camp and agreed to put Toghrul back on his throne. In the fighting that followed, Erke Kara was defeated. Toghrul was restored to power. Once again, Genghis Khan had proven himself a loyal ally.

In the region to the southeast, Tatar tribesmen led by the chieftain Megujin were committing attacks on the Jin

Empire. This was the region that is today the northern part of the People's Republic of China. In 1196, the Jin emperor decided to defeat Megujin. Jin general Wan-yan Xiang called upon Toghrul to help in the fight. Toghrul gladly gathered his Kereit warriors. He also called upon his Mongol ally Genghis Khan to join him. Genghis Khan was pleased at this chance to attack the Tatars. After all, it was the Tatars who had poisoned his father. The Tatars were longtime enemies of the Mongols.

In the winter of 1196, Toghrul and Genghis Khan started out with their warriors. While the Jin attacked the Tatars from the southeast, Toghrul and Genghis Khan attacked from the west. The Tatars were surprised in their camp. Megujin was captured and killed, along with many of his soldiers. The victory was swift and complete.

As he rode through the Tatar camp, Genghis Khan found a small orphan boy wearing a ring through his nose. He decided to take the boy home and give him to his mother to raise. Hoelun named the boy Shigi Khutukhu. This boy, Shigi Khutukhu, became Genghis Khan's adopted brother.

After the battle, Toghrul and Genghis Khan rode to the camp of the Jin general Wan-yan Xiang. The two men received honors from him for their service. He gave Toghrul the Chinese title Wang, or Prince. From then on, Toghrul was always known as Wang Khan. The Mongols pronounced the name as Ong Khan. Genghis Khan was rewarded with the lower title, Jaukhuri (Military Commander of the Frontier).[7] Genghis Khan, after all, was regarded as a follower of Ong Khan.

DEFEATING THE JURKIN

Genghis Khan realized he must still struggle with Jamuka for control of all of the Mongols. The riches he had captured from the Tatars attracted more followers. Genghis Khan believed he was now strong enough to conquer smaller Mongol clans. One of these clans was the Jurkin clan. It was located immediately to the south of Genghis Khan's territory along the Kerulen River. When he had agreed to fight the Tatars, Genghis Khan had called upon the Jurkin to help. But the Jurkin failed to honor his request. No Jurkin soldiers joined the Mongols on the march against the Tatars. In fact, while he was away, they raided Genghis Khan's own camp, killing ten of his guards. As a result, Genghis Khan swore he would punish them.

He set off on his campaign against the Jurkin in 1197. Swiftly he defeated them. It was then that Genghis Khan called for a second great change in the way he ruled his people. His first great change had been to appoint his most loyal and skilled followers to important positions. It did not matter if they were of noble blood or not. The second great change he decided on was a new way to deal with defeated enemies. Before, the camps of defeated tribes had been looted. Captured enemy warriors were made prisoners. Usually enough of the enemy people escaped to reorganize and remain free. They remained strong enough to cause trouble again at a later date. After defeating the Jurkin, however, Genghis Khan called for a kuriltai of his followers. At the kuriltai, he put Jurkin leaders on public trial. Those leaders found guilty of crimes were put to death. Afterward, Genghis Khan occupied the Jurkin lands. All surviving Jurkins were mixed among the families of his own clan.

In this way, Genghis Khan brought the defeated Jurkin into his tribe. He declared that they were not slaves. They were to be considered the equals of the Mongols. The Tatar boy Shigi Khutukhu was not the first war orphan Genghis Khan had adopted. After earlier wars, he had brought boys home from the defeated Merkit, Taijiut, and Tatar tribes. Publicly he had accepted the boys as his younger brothers. He demanded other families do the same. In this way, the Mongols became greater in numbers and strength. Genghis Khan had shown that he would treat his faithful followers well. Those who resisted his rule, however, would receive no mercy.

THE WRESTLING MATCH

After the Jurkin war, Genghis Khan found an opportunity to take revenge on a Jurkin named Buri-boko. His name actually meant "The Wrestler" or "The Strongman." Buri-boko was famous for his wrestling skills. At a feast, he once had had a drunken argument with Genghis Khan's half brother Belgutei. During the argument, Buri-boko had cut Belgutei's shoulder with a sword.

Now, Genghis Khan ordered that Buri-boko and Belgutei should have a wrestling match. Buri-boko was an undefeated champion. However, he did not dare to win this time. He let Belgutei throw him. Belgutei then grabbed Buri-boko by the shoulders and plunged his knee

43

MONGOL WRESTLING

Wrestling has been Mongolia's most popular sport since the times of Genghis Khan. Genghis Khan's own great-granddaughter, Qutulum, became famous as a wrestler. Modern Mongol wrestling matches are always held outdoors on grass. The wrestlers begin in standing positions. A wrestler loses when his body (from hips to shoulders), his knees, or his elbows touch the ground. Wrestling matches are held on religious and national holidays. A single match can last as long as four hours.[8]

into his back. The force of the sudden blow snapped Buri-boko's spine. Buri-boko's dying words were: "Belgutei could never have beaten me. For fear of the Khan I . . . allowed myself to be thrown. . . ."[9]

WARS ON THE STEPPES

"Genghis Khan," *The Secret History* tells us, "destroyed the leadership of the Jurkin clan . . ."[10] During the next few years, Genghis Khan and his ally Ong Khan fought several wars on the steppes. Sometimes they fought together. Sometimes they took on their enemies separately.

In the autumn of 1197, the Year of the Snake, Genghis Khan joined Ong Khan in a campaign against the chief Tokto'a-beki of the Merkit tribe. After the war, Genghis Khan presented all of the riches his troops had captured to Ong Khan as proof of his continued loyalty.

In 1198, the Year of the Horse, without discussing his plans with Genghis Khan, Ong Khan attacked the Merkits again. Ong Khan kept all of the captured loot for himself. Genghis Khan was angered by Ong Khan's greed, but still he remained loyal to his ally.

Ong Khan's greatest enemy was the Naiman tribe. In 1199, Inancha Bilge, the khan of the Naiman, died. His territories were divided between his two sons: Taibuka and Buyruk. Taibuka ruled the southwestern part of the kingdom. Buyruk ruled the area of the Altai Mountains. Genghis Khan and Ong Khan took advantage of this divided situation to attack Buyruk. Buyruk fled the region, leaving most of his army under the command of the chieftain Kokse'u Sabrak. Kokse'u Sabrak set an ambush for Genghis Khan and Ong Khan. Only too late did Genghis Khan and Ong Khan realize they had marched into a trap.

As the sun set, Genghis Khan and Ong Khan placed their troops in defensive position. They would fight their battle the next morning. Facing defeat, however, Ong Khan secretly retreated during the night. According to *The Secret History*, "During the night the Ong Khan lit false fires where his camp had been and went off . . ."[11]

Genghis Khan woke up in the morning and discovered Ong Khan had deserted him. There was nothing left to do but try to escape. He ordered his troops to mount their horses. In good order, they galloped away, and most of them escaped into the mountains.

Kokse'u Sabrak chose to chase after Ong Khan. He captured half of Ong Khan's fleeing army. In shock, Ong

Khan sent Genghis Khan a message, begging for help. Even though Ong Khan had treated him poorly, Genghis Khan refused to abandon his ally. He immediately sent soldiers to aid him, commanded by four of his best generals. Genghis Khan had always been loyal to Ong Khan. He had vowed to treat him with respect. He would not break his alliance now. With the help of Genghis Khan's soldiers, Ong Khan was able to defeat the Naiman.

In 1200, Genghis Khan and Ong Khan made an attack upon the Taijiut and defeated them. The Kereits enslaved the prisoners they took. Genghis Khan, however, continued his policy of taking captured warriors into his own army. Instead of making them slaves, he let them remain soldiers. In this way, Genghis Khan's army grew.

JAMUKA BECOMES GUR KHAN

Genghis Khan's growing power alarmed many of the independent Mongol clans on the central Asian steppes. By 1201, on the banks of the Ergune River, Jamuka united his own Jadaran clan with the Taijiuts, the Saljiuts, and half a dozen other independent Mongol clans. He also persuaded Tatar, Merkit, and Naiman warriors to join him. At a kuriltai, they elected Jamuka to become Gur Khan, which meant "Universal Lord."[12] Together, they formed an alliance. They swore an oath that they would attack Genghis Khan and Ong Khan.

Jamuka rode off at the head of his army to attack Genghis Khan. Genghis Khan sent riders to Ong Khan to warn him. At the same time, he prepared to wage war.

When Ong Khan joined him, they rode together down the Kerulen River. Genghis Khan's and Ong Khan's troops suddenly appeared before Jamuka's army at a place called Koyiten.

THE BATTLE OF KOYITEN

According to *The Secret History*, one of the commanders in Jamuka's army tried to conjure magic to help at Koyiten. He called for a thunderstorm to destroy the armies of Genghis Khan and Ong Khan. It was believed that some people had magical skills and this commander was one of them. The next day, a terrific thunderstorm did indeed pour down rain. However, the storm fell on Jamuka's soldiers instead of on his enemies. Jamuka's soldiers found themselves struggling to move in knee-deep mud. Jamuka's allies decided to abandon him, and they rode away. There was nothing left for Jamuka to do but retreat with his remaining troops.

Jamuka's alliance was crushed. The clans scattered in all directions. While Ong Khan chased after Jamuka, Genghis Khan ordered his horsemen to ride after the Taijiuts. His army crossed the Onon River and caught up with the fleeing Taijiuts. Genghis Khan learned that Targutai, the chief of the Taijiuts, was planning an attack. Although outnumbered, Genghis Khan's warriors held their ground. From horseback, the enemy armies sent arrows flying through the air at one another. The battle lasted all day long. The fight was still undecided as the sun began to set. Then, an arrow struck Genghis Khan in the neck.

FAITHFUL JELME

The warriors of the steppes often used poisoned arrows. Genghis Khan might have died of his neck wound, if it had not been for his faithful officer Jelme. During the night, Jelme saved Genghis Khan by sucking the poison from the wound. He would fill his mouth with the blood he sucked out and then spit it on the ground. At midnight, Genghis Khan regained his senses for a moment. He was very thirsty and begged for a drink. Jelme promised to do what he could.

Jelme stripped off his clothes and crept across the battlefield. He sneaked into the enemy camp and searched for fermented mare's milk. This was the drink the Mongol's often drank called kumiss. Jelme could not find any kumiss, however. But he did find a leather goat skin that contained curdled milk. Slowly and carefully, he made his way across the battlefield again. He brought the curdled milk back to camp. Mixed with water, he made a drink that he let Genghis Khan sip.

The Taijiut did not know that Genghis Khan had been wounded. During the night, many exhausted Taijiut warriors snuck away from the battlefield. When the sun rose, it was discovered that most of the Taijiut had fled. Genghis Khan felt well enough to send his warriors in pursuit. The Taijiut chieftain Targutai was killed. Many of the Taijiut were captured. The moment had arrived for Genghis Khan to take revenge. He had never forgotten how the Taijiut had made him a prisoner and forced him to wear a cangue across his shoulders. He ordered that all captured Taijiut warriors be put to death. During the fight, he also paid an old debt. He saved the daughter of the Suldus man Sorqan-Shira. It was Sorqan-Shira who had helped young Genghis Khan escape from his cangue and Targutai's camp so many years before.

JEBEI, THE ARROW

After defeating the Taijiut, Genghis Khan brought all of the captured warriors before him. To this gathering, he made an announcement. Before the fight at Koyiten, he had been arranging his troops in battle line. It was then that an enemy soldier shot an arrow from a distant hilltop. The arrow had struck and killed Genghis Khan's warhorse. Now, Genghis Khan demanded to know, "Who was it that, shooting from the top of the ridge, broke the neck-bone of my horse?"[13]

In response to this demand, a horseman of the Besut clan galloped forward. He halted before Genghis Khan. Jumping down from his horse, he threw himself at the conqueror's feet. His name was Jirgadei, and he declared that he had shot the arrow. Jirgadei knew his life was at stake. He offered to become a loyal Mongol soldier, if Genghis Khan would only spare him.

Genghis Khan was famous among the Mongols for being a fair ruler. It was known that he greatly respected courage and honesty. Genghis Khan gazed at the young man a while before speaking. According to *The Secret History*, he finally declared, "When an enemy wishes to kill someone, he keeps the fact secret. But you have been

Mongol archers helped to cut down the enemy before their attack could even reach the Mongol front line. Here, a modern Mongolian man demonstrates a Mongol warrior's shooting style.

[honest] with me. Become, therefore, my companion. In memory of your deed, I will name you [Jebei]."[14] In the Mongol language, Jebei was the word for arrowhead. This brave young soldier Jebei would become one of Genghis Khan's most valued generals.

THE DEFEAT OF THE TATARS

In 1202, the Year of the Dog, Genghis Khan marched eastward on a new campaign against the Tatars. The victory over Jamuka's allied army and the complete defeat of the Taijiut clan had sparked a new desire in Genghis Khan. He had become the most powerful leader of the

Mongol people. Now he wished to rule everyone who lived on the Mongolian steppe. The Tatars had always been a dangerous enemy along the eastern border. By the spring of 1202, Genghis Khan felt strong enough to attack the Tatars. On the night before the battle, he gave the following order to his officers. "If we are victorious, you shall not seek for [loot]; when all is over it will be divided into equal shares."[15]

This order was another complete change in the laws that had long governed steppe life. Before, when raiding an enemy camp, attackers usually let the enemy warriors escape. Instead of chasing after them, they stopped to loot the abandoned camps. The people of the steppes had always fought for personal gain. The retreating enemy warriors were often able to reorganize and return for a counterattack. In this new war against the Tatars, however, Genghis Khan gave this new order. There would be no looting by his soldiers until total victory had been won. Genghis Khan claimed everything taken from conquered enemies. After a battle was finished, he personally would reward his soldiers as he thought fit.

In the fight against the Tatars, Genghis Khan's soldiers scored a complete success. Genghis Khan ordered death for every captured Tatar male who stood taller than the hub of a cart wheel. This was the Mongol measure of adulthood. The women and young children he divided among his people. Genghis Khan wanted the surviving Tatars taken in as full members of his tribe, not as slaves. To stress this, he adopted another Tatar child for his mother. He also encouraged his soldiers to marry Tatar women. As an example, he took two Tatar sisters, Yesugen and Yisui, as new wives for himself.

Genghis Khan also demanded that the widows and orphans of each of his killed soldiers receive a share of the loot. This order made his soldiers even more loyal to him. They understood that if they died in battle he would look after their families. In this way, Genghis Khan won the complete loyalty of his soldiers.

THE CONQUEST OF MONGOLIA

IN 1203, THE YEAR AFTER CONQUERING THE Tatar tribe, Genghis Khan ordered that his Mongol armies be reorganized again. An army of ten thousand was called a *tumen*. A tumen consisted of ten battalions of one thousand men each. Each battalion contained ten companies of one hundred men each. Each company had ten squads of ten men each. His warriors, no matter which clan or tribe they came from, were ordered into squads together. They were to fight side by side as equal comrades. Every soldier was made to promise he would never leave a fellow soldier behind in battle as a prisoner. Genghis Khan chose the leader of each tumen himself. By mixing his troops in this way, his followers became one united people.

THE END OF AN ALLIANCE

After years of battling alongside Ong Khan, Genghis Khan believed he had earned the right to be accepted as Ong

53

Khan's equal. Therefore, he suggested a marriage alliance. Genghis Khan offered his oldest son Jochi as a husband to one of Ong Khan's daughters. At the same time, he offered one of his daughters as a wife for Ong Khan's son Senggum.

Senggum refused to consider Genghis Khan's offer. He believed Genghis Khan had grown too strong. In his view, Genghis Khan and his Mongol followers were becoming a threat to the Kereit tribe. In 1203, Senggum met with ambassadors sent by Jamuka and the leaders of other independent steppe clans. Senggum agreed to join forces with these warriors. He told his father of his decision to become an enemy of Genghis Khan.

Ong Khan had to make a difficult choice. Genghis Khan had always been a loyal supporter, and Ong Khan did not think he could trust Jamuka. But Senggum insisted Genghis Khan was the greatest danger to the Kereits. "Even now, while you are still alive," Senggum told his father, "[Genghis Khan] leaves us no power. When, my Lord and father, you are very old, will he permit us to rule your people . . . ?"[1] In the end, Ong Khan decided to turn against Genghis Khan.

Senggum developed a plan to destroy Genghis Khan once and for all. Genghis Khan would be tricked into coming to the Kereit camp and then seized. Ong Khan agreed to this plan. A rider soon carried a message to Genghis Khan. In the message, Ong Khan invited Genghis Khan to come to his camp. They would celebrate the weddings Genghis Khan wanted.

Genghis Khan was excited that his marriage offers had been accepted. He hurriedly rode off for Ong Khan's camp. He only took with him his son Jochi and a bodyguard of ten men. He was usually much more careful. During the journey, they spent a night at the camp of old Monglik. He had been one of Yesugei's most loyal followers. Monglik warned Genghis Khan that Senggum could not be trusted. Genghis Khan considered this warning. Suddenly, he realized he was falling into a trap. He swiftly turned back toward the safety of his camp.

THE KEREITS ATTACK

When Genghis Khan failed to show up at the Kereit camp, Senggum understood that his plot had failed. He and Ong Khan quickly ordered their Kereit warriors to make a surprise attack on the Mongols. Senggum's allies, including Jamuka, would join them. Altogether, Senggum and Ong Khan led about fifteen thousand horsemen.[2]

Two Mongol horse herders, Badai and Kishlik, learned of the Kereit plans. They hurried ahead to warn Genghis Khan. They found Genghis Khan camped at Kalakaljit-elet near the headwaters of the Kalka River. Although warned, Genghis Khan had fewer than five thousand warriors with him in his camp.[3] It was too late to avoid battle. The Kereits attacked that very night. Genghis Khan's desperate soldiers successfully held off the attack. The Kereits stopped fighting when Senggum was struck in the cheek by an arrow.

During the night, Genghis Khan ordered his warriors to retreat. The Mongols had suffered heavy losses. Genghis Khan's son Ogodei was missing. The Mongols retreated a short distance and then waited. Genghis Khan refused to retreat farther away until he knew what had become of his son. At last, Ogodei was brought back to his father by Bo'orchu. Blood poured from a wound in Ogodei's leg. Genghis Khan now continued to withdraw. His son would recover, but only about half of Genghis Khan's troops had survived to follow him.

Genghis Khan and his men retreated eastward. Before the foothills of the Khingan Mountains, near the Kalka River, an enemy force commanded by Jamuka caught up with them. Genghis Khan's soldiers fiercely defended themselves, but Jamuka's army was too great. Again, Genghis Khan had to retreat in the dark of night. His battered army fled farther east, to the very edge of Mongolia.

DEFEATING THE KEREIT

Genghis Khan halted beside the salt marshes of Lake Baljuna. He discovered that only nineteen warriors remained at his side. The Mongol leader and his followers drank a toast of muddy water. Genghis Khan vowed that he would remember their loyalty always.

During the summer of 1203, Genghis Khan pastured his horses and nursed his wounded at Lake Baljuna. He also made plans for further battle. He had been defeated, but he would not give up. Genghis Khan sent riders to gather those of his followers who were scattered across the steppe. Loyal soldiers began arriving from all directions. By the end of the summer, Genghis Khan was strong enough to head westward, back toward Kereit territory.

Genghis Khan made a hurried march and fell upon the Kereits while they were feasting. Three days and nights of fierce fighting and the Kereit army was crushed. Ong Khan escaped westward into the territory of the Naiman empire. In this foreign land, he was stopped by a Naiman officer. The officer did not recognize the ruler of the Kereit tribe. He ordered Ong Khan killed. Senggum escaped into the Gobi Desert. He passed westward through the mountains, but was later captured and killed. Jamuka galloped westward into Naiman territory, too. He would continue to plot against his anda, Genghis Khan.

VICTORY

Genghis Khan had regained his power as a leader. He had retaken his Mongol territory. He had also conquered the Kereit kingdom. When he had conquered the Tatars and the Taijiut, he had completely destroyed them. The Kereit people, however, he enslaved. Lives of slavery would be his punishment for the followers of Ong Khan and Senggum.

Genghis Khan did not forget the two herdsmen who had warned him of the approaching enemy. "To Badai and Kishlik," he declared, "I give the golden palace tent of Ong-khan."[4] In addition to this reward, he made the two horse herders royal servants with special privileges.

By 1204, Genghis Khan had succeeded in becoming ruler of all the Mongol tribes.

Genghis Khan's victory over the Kereits made him the most powerful leader on the steppes. The medieval Arab writer Al-'Umari noted that Genghis Khan sent out messages to the Mongol clans "informing them of his views, his justice, laws and generosity . . ."[5] He let it be known that all people would be treated fairly, if they joined him. By 1204, the Year of the Rat, the last of the independent Mongols clans, the Oirats and Onggirat, agreed by treaty to join the Mongol army. Genghis Khan had become total master of most of central and eastern Mongolia.

CONQUEST OF THE NAIMAN

The Naiman remained the only people of the central Asian steppe left to challenge the rule of Genghis Khan. Tayang Khan was the leader of the Naiman. It was to Tayang Khan that Jamuka had fled for protection.

Tayang Khan's mother Gurbesu had no respect for the Mongols. According to *The Secret History*, she declared, "The [Mongols] have an unpleasant scent and wear black clothes. They live far away and long may they remain distant!"[6] Under his mother's influence, Tayang Khan prepared to fight the Mongols. Genghis Khan soon learned of these enemy plans from spies. In 1204, he marched out to fight the Naiman. It was a long 700 mile (1,126 kilometer) march westward before the Mongols reached the Naiman border at Sa'ari Ke'er. The Naiman army was supported by Merkit warriors commanded by Tokto-a-beki, Jadaran horsemen led by Jamuka, as well as other renegade soldiers of the Dorbet, Katagin, and Seljiut Mongol clans. Tayang Khan had a combined army much larger than Genghis Khan's. In addition, the horses of the Mongol army were in poor condition after the long march.

Dodai Cherbi, one of his Mongol officers, suggested a plan to Genghis Khan: "We are few in numbers," he explained, "and are [tired] by our long march. Let us rest here . . . and graze our horses until they have recovered. But to mislead the enemy, let us in the daytime [set out] a large number of dummies and order that during the night each man light five separate fires."[7] A dummy is a figure, often clothes stuffed with straw, designed to look like a human being. Dodai Cherbi's suggestion pleased Genghis Khan. That night, the Naiman saw the lights of campfires all over the steppe. Tayang Khan saw the twinkling lights and exclaimed, "They have more campfires than there are stars in the sky."[8]

Completely fooled, Tayang Khan decided to withdraw his army across the Altai Mountains. Tayang Khan's son remained and made an attack that failed. These Naiman soldiers soon joined Tayang Khan's retreat. Genghis Khan followed the Naiman enemy closely. His Mongols picked at the Naiman army with small, but constant, hit-and-run attacks. The Mongols called such hit-and-run attacks "the Moving Bush." They used a second method of attack, as well. It was called "the Lake Formation." In the Lake Formation, a long line of troops advanced, shot its arrows, and was immediately followed by the next line behind it. Like waves on the shore of a lake, the lines struck and then swiftly disappeared. Each line returned to the rear and formed for another attack. Great numbers of the Naiman were killed because of Genghis Khan's brilliant Lake Formation attack.

THE BATTLE OF CHAKIRMA'UT

The Naiman retreated into the Altai Mountains. At last, they found themselves climbing the steep cliffs of the mountain Chakirma'ut. Still, the Mongols chased after them. Tayang Khan saw four Mongol generals leading the enemy below him. They were Jebei, Kublai, Jelme, and Subodei. According to *The Secret History*, Tayang Khan turned to Jamuka and asked, "Who are these, that pursue our men, in the manner of wolves pursuing a flock of sheep . . . ?" Jamuka responded:

> They are the four hounds of my Temujin, fed on human flesh; he keeps them leashed on an iron chain; their skulls are of brass, their teeth are hewn in the rock, their tongues are like [knives], their hearts of iron. . . . they ride with the wind; in battle they [eat] human flesh. Now they have been unleashed; their spittle runs; they are full of joy.[9]

There was no truth in these descriptions, but they served to fill Tayang Khan with proper awe of the fearsome generals.

The Naiman were forced to retreat farther up the mountain. Tayang Khan turned to Jamuka again. "Who is that behind them, like a hungry hawk, impatient to advance?" Jamuka told him, "That is my *anda* Temujin, clad from head to foot in iron armor; he has flown [here] like a hungry vulture; do you see him?"[10]

61

At last, the Naiman had retreated to the very top of the mountain. They could retreat no farther. Here, Tayang Khan demanded that his troops stand and fight. They did their best, but they were no match for the advancing Mongols.

During the night, the Naiman attempted to escape. It was dark because there was no moon that night. The only way to escape was down the steep mountainside. In the darkness, many Naiman soldiers fell from the rocky trails to their deaths. *The Secret History* tells us their corpses piled up like "rotten logs" at the foot of the mountain.[11]

Jamuka was one who managed to escape. The following morning, the Mongol forces easily defeated the last of the Naiman. Tayang Khan was found wounded and dying.

The Battle of Chakirma'ut marked the end of the Naiman nation. Genghis Khan took Tayang Khan's mother, Gurbesu, prisoner. When she was first brought before him, he mocked, "Did you not say that the Mongols had a bad scent! Why then have you come to me?"[12]

DEFEAT OF THE MERKITS

The Naiman had been completely defeated. The entire tribe was enslaved by the Mongols. Only one great tribe remained as an immediate threat to the growing Mongol Empire. This tribe was the Merkits, located in the forests to the north of the steppes. The leader of the Merkits was named Toktoa.

UYGUR WRITING

After the defeat of the Naiman in 1204, a captured prisoner, Tata Tonga of the Uygur tribe, was brought before Genghis Khan. He carried something Genghis Khan had never seen before. It was Tayang Khan's official seal of office. Tata Tonga described the use of the seal, and the meaning of the Uygur letters written on it. Genghis Khan could not read or write. In fact, the Mongols had never had an alphabet or written language. Genghis Khan immediately recognized the value of writing. He appointed Tata Tonga his Keeper of the Seal. He ordered Tata Tonga to teach his sons how to read and write the Uygur script. The oldest piece of Mongol writing to survive today was carved on a stone in 1226. It marks the record distance Genghis Khan's nephew Yisungge shot an arrow. The distance was about 575 yards (525 meters).[13]

In the autumn of 1204, the Year of the Rat, Genghis Khan marched north at the head of his army. In bloody battle, the Merkit enemy was defeated. Toktoa fled with his beaten soldiers, and Genghis Khan chased after them. In time, the Mongol horsemen caught up with the Merkits at the Irtysh River, in the foothills of the Altai Mountains. In a second battle, the Mongols crushed the last of the Merkits and killed Toktoa.

After the fight, Genghis Khan's son Jochi wished to spare the life of one of Toktoa's brave sons. "Considering 'no tribe more wicked than the Merkit,' Genghis Khan refused Jochi's request." He insisted, "There is no better place for an enemy of our nation than the grave!"[14] All of the surviving Merkits were forced to join the Mongol nation. Genghis Khan took from among the Merkits his fourth wife, Kulan. His victory over the Merkits made him ruler of all of northern Mongolia. In every direction, the grassy high plateau was now Mongol territory, under the rule of Genghis Khan.

THE END OF JAMUKA

Genghis Khan's boyhood anda Jamuka still remained a threat to his power. Jamuka of the Jadaran clan once had been a feared khan of the Mongols. When Genghis Khan defeated the Naiman, Jamuka's allied army had been destroyed. By 1205, only five followers remained at Jamuka's side. They had found a hiding place in the Tannu Mountains and lived as a gang of robbers. As time passed, however, Jamuka's followers decided he might be worth more to them as a prisoner than as a leader.

One day in 1205, Jamuka and his men killed a wild sheep. In the evening, they sat around their fire and watched it cook. It was then that Jamuka's men seized him and tied him up. They hoped to receive a reward for presenting their leader to Genghis Khan. Jamuka's men brought him to the camp of the great khan. However, they did not receive the welcome they had expected. Genghis Khan was a man who greatly believed in loyalty. According to *The Secret History*, he exclaimed, "Is it possible to leave alive men who have betrayed their own lord! Let them be put to death, with their sons and grandsons."[15] Instead of receiving a reward, the men had their heads cut off.

Next, Genghis Khan had to decide what to do with Jamuka. Jamuka was still his anda, his blood brother. To the Mongols, the killing of an anda was a terrible crime. For a time, Genghis Khan thought this problem over. In the end, Jamuka himself gave Genghis Khan the solution. He told Genghis Khan that there was no other choice but to kill him. "If you do not," Jamuka admitted, "I shall always be like a louse on your collar. . . . Because of me you will be uneasy by day, and at night will sleep fitfully."[16]

With a feeling of sadness, Genghis Khan had his anda put to death. He executed Jamuka in the most respectful way he could. According to Mongol religion, a person's soul was in his blood. Therefore, a bloodless death was considered the kindest way to die. With this in mind, Genghis Khan had Jamuka rolled into a rug and crushed to death. Jamuka's blood was not shed. With the death of Jamuka, there was no one left on the steppes to challenge the great Genghis Khan.

Under the Eternal Blue Sky

GENGHIS KHAN RETURNED TO THE HEADWATERS of the Onon River near the sacred mountain of Burkhan Khaldun. In 1206, the Year of the Tiger, he called for a kuriltai to gather there. All of the steppe clans rode to the great encampment. They raised their yurts in great circles, until they grew into a city of tents. Before Genghis Khan's yurt stood a white pole. Its tip was decorated with nine white yak tails. Each tail represented one of the great Mongol clans.

The People of the Felt Walls

At the kuriltai, forty-four-year-old Genghis Khan declared that all of the people he had conquered were now united as one. From then on, even the great tribes like the Kereit and

66

the Naiman were to call themselves Mongols. Genghis Khan named his people "Yeke Mongol Ulus," which meant in the Mongol language "the Great Mongol Nation."[1] He also called his nomad subjects "the People of the Felt Walls."[2]

In every Mongol camp there were men called shamans. The shamans claimed they had magical skills. They were nearly as respected and influential as tribal leaders. The Mongols listened to their shamans on all important occasions. It was believed a shaman could tell the future and calm evil spirits. It was thought he could use his powers to control the weather or to bring victory in battle. In 1206, the most respected Mongol shaman was Kokochu. Kokochu was the son of Monglik, who had been Yesugei's loyal servant. Kokochu was best known by his religious title Teb Tengri, which meant "Most Heavenly."[3]

Teb Tengri played a part at the 1206 kuriltai. He declared that he had ridden into heaven on a spotted gray

READING BONES

Among the Mongols, it was believed shamans could see into the future. One method shamans used was the reading of bones. A shaman would take a sheep's shoulder blade and whisper a question to it. Then the bone was put into a fire until it was burned and cracked. The shaman next would carefully examine, or read, the bone to find the answer to his whispered question. A vertical crack across the bone meant the answer was yes. A horizontal crack across the bone meant the answer was no.[4]

horse and spoken to God. He claimed the Eternal Blue Heaven had appointed Genghis Khan as his representative on earth. Genghis Khan gladly accepted this belief. "The Sky has ordered me to govern all peoples," he said.[5]

During the kuriltai, Genghis Khan ordered that a census of the Mongol people be taken. Chief judge Shigi Khutukhu was put in charge of making the official count. It was recorded that there were ninety-five thousand Mongol households or families altogether.[6]

At the kuriltai, the Mongols celebrated the founding of their new nation. They drank foaming kumiss from cow-horn cups. People sang and danced in circles. On a great throne in his chieftain's yurt, Genghis Khan sat with his first wife Borte. His four sons and other relatives sat on lower seats. Tribe and clan noblemen joined in the grand feast in honor of this new era in their history.

REORGANIZING THE MONGOL ARMY

Genghis Khan rewarded his loyal soldiers for their years of service. He gave them gifts of cattle and money. During the kuriltai, he also continued the reorganization of his people. All males from the ages of fifteen to seventy were ordered to train as soldiers. Any man who left his assigned unit was condemned to death. This military reorganization greatly influenced the entire structure of the Mongol nation. Genghis Khan let only the people of his most loyal allies stay together. The Oirats and the Onggirat were allowed to remain as clans, for example. They had voluntarily joined in alliance with Genghis Khan. When he was done reorganizing, Genghis Khan had created an army of nearly one hundred thousand cavalrymen.[7]

The Mongol army was based on a system of tens. A small guard of ten horsemen was called an *arban*, the word for ten in the Mongol language. The largest unit of ten thousand troops was called a *tumen*, the Mongol word for ten thousand. Each tumen was commanded by a general Genghis Khan selected himself. He chose his most loyal and skilled officers. His military leaders were completely faithful to him. Any commander who failed to perform his duties well could lose his position and be put on trial. One of Genghis Khan's orders was recorded by the Persian writer Rashid ad-Din. It declared, "If a troop commander is unable to keep his troop ready for battle he [and his family] will all be arraigned and another leader will be selected from within the troop."[8]

Genghis Khan also made his personal bodyguard much larger. It had once numbered one hundred fifty men. Now he commanded, "Since Heaven has ordered me to rule all nations, 10,000 men shall form my guard."[9] The soldiers in his bodyguard included the sons and brothers of his generals.

There was plenty of work for Mongol men who did not become soldiers. The old, the young, and men badly scarred by battle injuries all had duties to perform. Some guarded the herds and flocks. Others made bows and arrows. Still others trained horses. Every Mongol knew he or she was part of a nation of warriors.

MONGOL HORSEMEN

Mongol soldiers were all horsemen. They wore special clothes and carried special equipment when riding into combat. Each man wore a metal helmet. An attached leather guard hung down from the helmet to protect his neck and ears. On his body, he wore thick armor made from layers of buffalo leather. It covered his shoulders, chest, and back. Additional leather guard pieces protected his arms and legs.

Each Mongol cavalryman carried several weapons and tools on his horse. He had two quivers, in order to carry two different kinds of arrows. Lightweight arrows could fly great distances through the air. Heavier arrows were used in close combat to do more damage. Each horseman carried thirty arrows of each kind, as well as two bows. In addition, each rider carried a lance with a sharp hook behind the point. The hook allowed him to yank an enemy from his horse. Mongol cavalrymen also carried axes, knives, swords, horsehair ropes, kettles, grindstones for sharpening arrowheads, and horsewhips.

All Mongol troops carried a leather water bag when riding. Extra food rations included about ten pounds of dried curds and dried mutton or beef. If a Mongol found himself without food and water, he could always cut his horse's jugular vein. After opening the vein in the horse's neck, he could suck out some blood to drink. Then he could close the wound by slapping grass on it. The horse did not suffer much from the experience.

CROSSING RIVERS

When the Mongols crossed wide rivers, they often put their clothes into leather sacks. When the sacks were tightly tied, they formed rounded cushions. The Mongols placed their saddles on these sacks and climbed on top of them. Then their horses were driven into the water by swimmers and guided toward the opposite shore. The Mongols seated on top of their floating sacks held onto their horses tails. The swimming horses pulled them across the rivers.

The Mongols used several tricks in order to fight successfully. To give an impression of strength, Mongol cavalry advanced side by side across a broad front. When a strong enemy force showed that it intended to fight, the Mongols often made a show of riding away in retreat. The enemy often followed the retreating Mongols. When the Mongols reached a place that favored attack, they suddenly turned and surprised their tired pursuers by fighting. Mongol armies marched with astonishing speed. They traveled light, without supply wagons. They carried whatever supplies they needed with them on horseback. They could march for ten days without stopping to cook food.

THE GREAT YASA AND THE BILIG

In 1206, Genghis Khan ordered that the laws of the Mongol Empire be collected in a book. This book was known as *The Great Yasa*. Genghis Khan understood that written laws would help his nation become stronger. *The Great Yasa* was written in the Uygur alphabet Genghis Khan had chosen to use. He also had a book written that contained his sayings. This book of words to live by was called the *Bilig*.

The Great Yasa recorded many ancient Mongol traditions, customs, and laws. Genghis Khan declared these all must be followed. He also added new laws of his own. He continued to add to *The Great Yasa* throughout his life. No complete copy of *The Great Yasa* is known today. Only fragments have survived.

It was said the first words Genghis Khan added to *The Great Yasa* outlawed the kidnapping of women. Genghis Khan had not forgotten the kidnapping of his own wife Borte so many years earlier. He also outlawed the stealing of horses, as well as common theft. Both of these crimes were to be punished by death. He outlawed the hunting of wild animals between March and October, too. That was the time of the year when young animals were born. Genghis Khan wished to make sure there would always be wild animals to hunt.

The Great Yasa contained moral, social, and religious laws. Genghis Khan demanded that total religious freedom be guaranteed for all of his people. He recognized that this was a way to keep the peace in his empire. To promote all religions, Genghis Khan refused to tax religious leaders or their property or religious institutions. No religious leader was required to serve in the army or perform public service. Later, Genghis Khan also granted these rights to such valued professionals as doctors, lawyers, and teachers.

The laws of *The Great Yasa* were designed to make the Mongol nation stronger and more kind. One law of *The Great Yasa* insisted, "Anyone who calls on people who are then eating shall, without asking permission, sit down and eat with them."[10] Genghis Khan's sayings in the *Bilig* often showed much wisdom. One saying in the *Bilig* declared, "Only a man who feels hunger and thirst . . . is fit to be a commander, as he will see that his warriors do not suffer from hunger and thirst and that the four-footed beasts do not starve."[11]

Genghis Khan made all of the decisions about how his people should behave. To keep track of his laws, he created the position of chief judge. He chose his adopted brother Shigi Khutukhu to become chief judge. Shigi Khutukhu was the Tatar boy with the nose ring whom his mother was given to raise in 1196. Genghis Khan told Shigi Khutukhu, "Now that I have assured my control over all nations, you shall be my ears and my eyes."[12] Shigi Khutukhu was to decide all cases and give punishment to those who deserved it. In order to avoid future challenges, Shigi Khutukhu was instructed to keep a written record of all of his decisions that had received approval from Genghis Khan.

THE ARROW MESSENGERS

For many years, the Mongols had used "arrow riders" to carry messages across great distances. This service was called the *Jam* in the Mongol language. It was much like the United States' Pony Express system of the 1850s.

Genghis Khan relied on the system of fast riders to bring him news. Relay stations were established about twenty miles apart. At the relay stations, riders could get fresh horses, food, and rest. There were about sixty-four relay stations across Mongolia.[13] They stretched from the Altai Mountains in the west to China's Great Wall in the east.

Genghis Khan's generals and district governors were expected to report every unusual event as fast as they could. Genghis Khan placed his general Jelme in charge of all of the arrow messengers. Each day riders galloped back and forth across the countryside. An arrow messenger's head and body were bandaged. This protected the rider from the sting of blowing sand during his long journeys. He rode his horse hard and often slept in the saddle. The arrow messenger service made sure that nothing could happen in all of Mongolia without Genghis Khan quickly learning about it.

CONTROL OF SIBERIA

By 1206, Genghis Khan ruled the greatest portion of present-day Outer Mongolia. He was the master of lands stretching from the Gobi Desert in the south to the frozen Arctic in the north. His word was law from the forests of Manchuria in the east to the Altai Mountains in the west.

In 1207, Genghis Khan continued his conquest of northwest Mongolia. He sent his oldest son, twenty-eight-year-old Jochi, to the region beyond Lake Baikal. At the head of an army, Jochi rode into Sibir. The modern name of Siberia comes from this name. The Oirat people of Sibir soon surrendered to Jochi without battle. Other tribes also peacefully agreed to join the Mongols. Before long, the Kirghiz, the Buriat, the Barqun, the Ursut, and the Tubas all promised to call Genghis Khan their leader.

THE CHALLENGE OF A SHAMAN

There was danger lurking in Genghis Khan's camp. The shaman Teb Tengri was ambitious and had great influence. He often gave Genghis Khan advice that he said had come from Heaven. As a religious leader, the shaman's power continued to grow. Teb Tengri and his six brothers sometimes even showed disrespect toward Genghis Khan's family.

One day, Teb Tengri's brothers gave Genghis Khan's brother Kasar a beating. They were not punished by Genghis Khan. Later, Teb Tengri told Genghis Khan that he had had a dream. He claimed he had seen a vision of Genghis Khan as the ruler of the Mongol nation. But after a second dream he warned that he had seen Kasar as Mongol ruler. He urged Genghis Khan to take action against his brother. Genghis Khan immediately had Kasar arrested.

Their mother, Hoelun, soon learned of Kasar's arrest. She hurried to Genghis Khan's yurt and saved Kasar from further danger. She shamed Genghis Khan into setting Kasar free. But the influence of Teb Tengri continued to increase.

75

Genghis Khan's wife Borte realized Teb Tengri was becoming dangerous. After the arrest and release of Kasar, Borte talked with her husband. According to *The Secret History*, she asked him, "What sort of an order are you establishing, when your own brothers cannot be sure of their lives? What sort of a Khan are you when you heed the words of a shaman?"[14] Genghis Khan finally realized his wife was right. He decided he must get rid of Teb Tengri.

It was not long afterward that Teb Tengri publicly insulted Genghis Khan's brother Temuge. This time, Genghis Khan told Temuge that he could deal with the shaman as he saw fit. Within days, Teb Tengri visited Genghis Khan's yurt. Temuge was there as well. An argument between Temuge and Teb Tengri soon started. Temuge gripped the shaman by the collar, and the two men struggled.

The Secret History reveals that Genghis Khan ordered that the argument be settled by a traditional contest of strength. "You two," he commanded, "go off and wrestle."[15] Outside the great khan's tent, Temuge had three strong men waiting. When Teb Tengri stepped outside, these men seized him and broke his spine. With this painful death, Teb Tengri was no longer a threat to Genghis Khan.

WAR WITH THE TANGUTS

In 1207, Genghis Khan found a new opportunity to use his great army. There were three powerful kingdoms to the south of the Mongol Empire. To the southeast lay the Jin

Empire. To the southwest, at the great bend of the Yellow River, lay the kingdom of the Tanguts. Even farther west could be found the kingdom of the Kara Khitai.

The Jin Empire had been created in 1125 by the conquering Jurchen tribe from Manchuria. The empire included much of the northern part of the present-day People's Republic of China. In Genghis Khan's time, a series of high walls separated much of the Mongol Empire from China. Each wall stretched many miles. Construction having begun around 200 B.C., the Jin hoped these walls would keep the Mongols out of their territory. In the fourteenth and fifteenth centuries, the Chinese would connect and improve many of these walls to create the Great Wall of China.

It was the Jin Empire that Genghis Khan wished most to conquer. There were great cities in China. Chinese factories and craftsmen manufactured jewelry, textiles, furniture, and other valued goods. The Mongols were not skilled metalworkers, weavers, or carpenters. The Mongols were a poor people, but they were great warriors. Genghis Khan wished to use the strength of his army to enrich his people.

Before launching an attack against the Jin Empire, Genghis Khan first looked to the southwest. The Tangut kingdom called Xi-Xia contained cities and riches like those found in the Jin Empire. The Tangut kingdom was located along the upper part of the Yellow River. Today the region is in the Gansu and Ningxia provinces of the People's Republic of China.[16] The Tanguts were not as powerful as the Jins. Therefore, Genghis Khan chose to

77

The Great Wall of China was built from many small walls constructed to help protect the Jin Empire from Mongols and other raiders.

attack them first. In 1207, he sent raiding parties to attack Tangut towns and cities. Soon, Genghis Khan himself marched southward with a small army. They crossed the Gobi Desert, digging wells for water as they went. Not even the high walls, some of which stretched across Tangut lands, could stop the Mongol advance.

The Mongol raids into Tangut territory taught Genghis Khan's troops new ways to fight. His soldiers had never had to capture walled cities and forts before. They quickly learned how to cut off Tangut citizens from food supplies in the surrounding countryside. They would surround a city and let no one in or out. This military tactic is called a siege. By 1209, Genghis Khan felt ready for a full scale war against the Tanguts. Again, the Mongol army marched 650 miles southward. The journey required that they cross the sands of the Gobi Desert. In May, the Mongols successfully attacked the Tangut city of Wulahai. But they suffered a defeat near a mountain pass when attacked by a Tangut army commanded by General Weiming-linggong.

In August, Genghis Khan decided to use a trick to defeat Weiming-linggong. The Mongols hurried away from their camp as if retreating. But, in truth, they stopped at a place from which they could ambush the enemy. Weiming-linggong marched his Tangut soldiers after the Mongols. Suddenly, they found themselves surrounded by the entire Mongol army. The Tangut army suffered a terrible defeat. Weiming-linggong was taken prisoner.

The remains of the Tangut army fled into the city of Ningxia on the Yellow River. The Mongol army surrounded Ningxia and began a siege. In October, Genghis Khan ordered that a large dam be built. It was designed so that autumn rains could be directed into the city and flood it.

The floodwaters drowned many Tanguts and destroyed many buildings. The Mongols, however, were not skilled dam builders. In January 1210, the dam suddenly burst. Floodwater poured through the Mongol camps outside the city. It forced the Mongols to retreat to higher ground. As a result, Genghis Khan realized he could not capture Ningxia. He decided to offer the Tanguts peace. The Tangut king, Li Anquan, was pleased to accept a peace treaty. He paid the Mongols many riches, including thousands of camels and many bolts of colorful silk cloth. He also gave Genghis Khan one of his daughters as a wife. The Tangut king sent Genghis Khan the following message: "Having heard of your glory . . . we were greatly afraid, but now we will be your right hand . . . and will serve you faithfully . . ."[17] Once more, Genghis Khan had brought a great nation under his control.

WAR AGAINST THE JIN EMPIRE

IN 1210, A JIN AMBASSADOR ARRIVED AT GENGHIS Khan's camp. He brought news that a new emperor had taken the throne of the Jin Empire. Genghis Khan had served the Jin during the Tatar wars. Now it was expected that he show his continuing loyalty. Normally, the news of a new Jin emperor would require that he make a low bow. The Chinese called such a bow a *kow tow*. Genghis Khan asked who the new emperor was. He was told that the Jin prince Yun-chi had taken the throne. When he learned this, Genghis Khan did not kow tow. Instead, he turned to the south and spit at the ground. "If an idiot can become the emperor," he declared, "it is hardly worth kow-towing to his messenger."[1] Then he mounted his horse and rode away.

MARCHING TO WAR

Genghis Khan's insult to the new Jin emperor was so great that it was regarded as a declaration of war. In March

81

1211, Genghis Khan held a kuriltai beside the Kerulen River. At the kuriltai, he made plans for war against the Jin Empire. Before starting this great war, Genghis Khan climbed the holy mountain Bhurkan Khaldun. Inside a tent on the mountaintop, he prayed for help from the Eternal Blue Heaven. The Persian historian Juzjani later wrote that on the fourth day Genghis Khan stepped from his tent and declared, "Heaven has promised me victory."[2]

The Mongol ruler left his youngest brother Temuge to protect Mongolia with a force of twenty thousand. With the rest of his great army, Genghis Khan set out southward. The first challenge of the Mongol army was the crossing of the Gobi Desert. Each Mongol cavalryman brought a spare horse for the 600-mile journey. Herds of cattle to provide food were also driven along. The Mongols also used camels to carry supplies across the sandy desert.

It is believed the Jin army numbered about six hundred thousand men. Genghis Khan had probably no more than sixty-five thousand of his own troops, as well as ten thousand Onggirat warriors."[3] Our empire is like the sea; yours is but a handful of sand," a Chinese historian noted the boastful Jin emperor declared. "How can we fear you?"[4] But the Mongols could move fast and were well-trained. Genghis Khan crossed the weakly defended border walls, and after a march of another 120 miles fell upon the rich Chinese province of Shan-si. Genghis Khan divided his forces into three armies commanded by his three oldest sons, Jochi, Chagatai, and Ogodei. The Mongol invaders spread out like a fan and invaded the rich province.

The Capture of Tung Ching

In the spring of 1212, the Mongols lay siege to the city of Tung Ching. After surrounding the city, Genghis Khan's general Jebei realized it would be a long time before it would surrender. Instead of a siege, he tried a favorite Mongolian military movement. He commanded his army to make a hurried retreat. His troops left loaded baggage wagons and tents standing outside the city walls. For two days, the Mongols retreated. Then, with fresh horses, they rushed back the entire distance to the city in a single night. As they had hoped, they discovered the Jin had opened the city gates. Many of the city troops were in the abandoned Mongol camp searching for loot. The Mongols rode down upon the surprised Jin soldiers and then galloped through the open city gates. Tung Ching was easily captured.

In the summer of 1212, the Mongols trapped another Jin army in a valley as the army marched to save the city of Xijing. During the siege of Xijing, Genghis Khan was struck by an arrow and badly wounded. The Mongol army fell back to the north, while their leader nursed his wound. By early August, the Mongols returned and the siege continued. The city surrendered before the month had ended.

Methods of Attack

Before attacking a city, the Mongols usually cleared out all of the surrounding villages. Mongol warriors rounded up the local Jin peasants. These prisoners were forced to do chores in the Mongol army camps. They cooked food, fetched water, and fed horses. They were also forced to move and operate the heavy siege machines. Men wheeled forward high wooden siege towers, so that archers could shoot arrows into a city. Catapults hurled stones or containers of flaming liquids over city walls. The ballista was a machine that shot giant arrows. The firelance was a bamboo tube filled with gunpowder. When it was lit, sparks and flames shot out of the tube like a flamethrower. This weapon was used to start fires and to frighten enemy soldiers and their horses.

Faced by a walled town, the Mongols would round up the women, children, and old people of the countryside. They would drive these people forward in front of them. No Jin soldiers would intentionally fire on their own people. Towns that immediately surrendered were spared, but those that fought were completely destroyed. The Mongol armies often attacked undefended villages and set them on fire. The frightened peasants fled in all directions. During the Jin war, more than a million refugees entered the cities in search of protection. Inside the cities, these refugees ate food supplies and spread fearful stories of the Mongol enemy.

In battle, the Mongols sometimes used "the Crow Swarm" or "Falling Stars" method of attack. At the signal of a drum, or by fire signal at night, the Mongol horsemen galloped at the enemy from all directions. One Jin witness exclaimed, "They come as though the sky were falling, and they disappear like the flash of lightning."[5] Before the surprised Jin could respond to one of these attacks, the Mongols already had disappeared again.

Squads of Mongol horsemen on patrol were sometimes surprised by the enemy. To save themselves, they would throw valuable items on the ground as they galloped away. The enemy would usually stop to pick up the goods. As a result, the Mongols were able to escape. At other times, escaping Mongols tossed sand into the wind or dragged tree branches from their horses' tails. In these ways, they raised great clouds of dust. The dust clouds hid their

The Mongols were skilled horsemen and often swarmed around their enemy in great numbers.

movements and made the enemy think there were more Mongols than there really were.

PEACE TERMS

With his youngest son Tolui at his side, Genghis Khan commanded the main Mongol army. His three oldest sons, Jochi, Chagatai, and Ogodei, took charge of a second army. A third army column was commanded by Genghis Khan's brothers, Kasar and Temuge. Before the end of December 1213, the three armies continued their march southward. By the spring of 1214, nearly all of the Jin lands north of the Yellow River had been captured by the Mongols. Only about a dozen walled cities, including the Jin "Middle Capital," Zhongdu (present-day Beijing), had not fallen to the Mongols.

In April 1214, Genghis Khan gathered his armies north of Zhongdu. Zhongdu was a huge city, eighteen miles in circumference.[6] The great walls of clay that surrounded the city stood forty feet high. Nine hundred towers gave additional protection along these walls. Three moats filled with water circled the city. There were also four strong forts outside the city walls. Inside Zhongdu, twenty thousand Jin soldiers were prepared to defend the city. Another four thousand troops stood guard in each of the four forts.[7]

Twice the Mongols attacked Zhongdu. Twice they were forced to fall back. In time, hunger, heat, and fever took their toll in the Mongol camps. Genghis Khan realized it would cost a great deal to conquer Zhongdu. Finally, he sent a messenger to the Jin emperor, Xuanzong. In his message, Genghis Khan declared, "All the provinces of your realm northward of the Yellow River are in my hands. You have nothing left but your capital. To this weakness Heaven has reduced you."[8] He then offered to march his soldiers away, if the Jin would give the Mongols a reward for doing so. The Jin emperor seized upon this opportunity to be rid of the Mongol enemy. He offered great bolts of silk and large sacks of gold, five hundred slaves, and three thousand horses to the Mongols. He also offered one of his daughters as a bride for Genghis Khan. In addition, he agreed to give Genghis Khan control of the northern Jin province of Liao. In May 1214, Genghis Khan accepted these peace terms.

The Mongol armies began the long journey back toward their homeland. *The Secret History* later noted, "They took away from Zhongdu as much as they could carry."[9] Genghis Khan withdrew to a summer camp in Mongolia. After three years of war, he left the Jin Empire in triumph. The strength of the Jin Empire had been broken. Genghis Khan now ranked as the greatest ruler in all of eastern Asia.

THE RETURN TO ZHONGDU

On the journey homeward, Genghis Khan camped with his troops at the southern edge of the Gobi Desert. At a place called "Dolon Nor" (Seven Lakes), they waited for the cool weather of autumn before trying to cross. While waiting, Genghis Khan learned that the Jin emperor

Xuanzong had moved his court southward from Zhongdu to the city of Kaifeng, south of the Yellow River. Upon learning this news, Genghis Khan grew very angry. He believed the Jin planned to gather a new army in the south and then return north to attack the Mongols. "The Jin Emperor," he exclaimed, "made a peace agreement with me, but now he has moved his capital to the south; evidently he mistrusts my word and has used the peace to deceive me."[10]

Genghis Khan believed the Jin had broken their treaty. He started his Mongol army marching southward again. In the spring of 1215, as the Mongols approached Zhongdu, many frightened Jin soldiers deserted their regiments and joined the Mongol forces.

THE CAPTURE OF ZHONGDU

In late spring of 1215, Genghis Khan halted his army in front of Zhongdu. He felt so sure of victory that he put Ming-an, a Khitan general in his army, in command of the siege. He himself returned to camp at Dolon Nor. As the days passed, the situation inside Zhongdu grew worse. A Jin relief force tried to bring supplies to the city. It was defeated by the Mongols. The hopeless commander of the city, Wayen Fuxing, poisoned himself soon after. Inside Zhongdu, food became so scarce that starving people became cannibals. They ate their dead neighbors.

At last, in June, the Mongols broke into the city. All of the gold in the government treasury was captured. Zhongdu suffered a month of looting. Fires broke out and

THE FAKE GENERAL

Shimo Yesen, a Khitan general, joined the Mongols in their war against the Jin. Shimo Yesen felt sure the capture of the northern Jin city of Liaoyang would greatly help the Mongols in their war. In 1215, Yesen planned a clever trick to capture Liaoyang. Yesen had learned that a new Jin general was to take over the defense of the city. He hid with a few Mongol cavalrymen on the road leading to the city. These horsemen captured and killed the new general before he could reach Liaoyang. Taking the general's official documents, Yesen boldly rode into the city. At the military headquarters, he announced that he was the new general sent to take command. He dismissed the city guard and appointed new officers. Three days later, the Mongols easily marched into the city. One hundred thousand Jin soldiers had been captured and not a single arrow had been shot.

burned many buildings. Thousands of Jin were massacred. The bones of the dead were heaped in great piles. The ancient Persian historian Baha al-Din Razi later wrote that near one of the city gates lay one huge mountain of bones. These were the remains of sixty thousand frightened girls who had thrown themselves from the walls. They committed suicide rather than become the slaves of the terrible Mongols.[11] It is uncertain whether this report is completely true or not.

The capture of Zhongdu greatly increased Genghis Khan's power. Few could argue that he had become the

89

strongest ruler in all of Asia. The Mongol armies continued to overrun Jin territories north of the Yellow River. Mongol soldiers also marched into the northeast part of the present-day People's Republic of China and captured Jin territory there. The Mongols forced Korea to pay tribute, too. In 1217, Genghis Khan appointed his general Mukali to command all Mongol forces in China. Mukali was ordered to carry on the war. As the war continued, the Mongols left their mark throughout northern China. Eight hundred towns and cities fell to Mukali's Mongol army.[12]

CHINESE TREASURE

For weeks after the capture of Zhongdu, caravans made their way northward toward Mongolia. Camels carried loads of silk and other valued cloth, painted furniture, porcelain bowls, metal armor, and bronze and iron pots and pans. Wagons carried bottles of perfume and chests filled with glittering jewelry. Oxen pulled carts piled high with kegs of wine, jars of honey, and boxes of spices. Great crowds of slaves were marched along as well. The Mongols carried home everything of value.

Some of the Chinese prisoners being marched along were craftsmen and scholars. One young man was named Yehlu Ch'u ts'ai. Yehlu Ch'u ts'ai was an educated Jin government official. Brought before Genghis Khan, he warned, "The Mongol Empire has been won from the saddle—it cannot be ruled from the saddle."[13] Many Mongol generals urged Genghis Khan to kill most of the northern Jin. Their lands could be used to graze horses and cattle. But Yehlu Ch'u ts'ai explained to Genghis Khan that the Mongol nation could tax the Jin people and gain money year after year. Genghis Khan agreed to let the Jin live. He gave Yehlu Ch'u ts'ai the power to govern the conquered Jin territory. Near the end of 1215, after being away for four and a half years, Genghis Khan returned to the Mongolian steppes.

CONQUEST OF THE KARA KHITAI

Genghis Khan had felt a need to return home in a hurry. He had learned that Kodu, a leader of the Merkit tribe, had gathered an army and was preparing to attack. In 1217, Genghis Khan sent an army to destroy the Merkits. In time, the Merkits were defeated. All of the captured Merkit soldiers were put to death.

Kuchlug, son of Tayang Khan of the Naiman, also had become a threat to the Mongols. He was gathering Naiman followers in Kara Khitai. Kara Khitai was the great territory west of the Altai Mountains. In 1218, Genghis Khan sent a Mongol army of twenty thousand men commanded by his general Jebei into the Kashgar region of Kara Khitai. Jebei promised the people of the region that their religions would be respected under Mongol rule. Kuchlug had heavily taxed and mistreated these people for practicing their Buddhist and Muslim religions. Rebellion soon broke out against Kuchlug's rule. Jebei led his Mongol army 2,500 hundred miles across the length of Asia and into Kara Khitai. The Mongol army soon defeated Kuchlug's troops. Kuchlug himself was captured and beheaded.

After his victory, Jebei cleverly sent home a sign of his loyalty. Genghis Khan received a gift of one thousand chestnut horses with white muzzles. Chestnut is a reddish-brown color, and the muzzle is the mouth of an animal. These gift horses had the same colorings as the horse that Jebei had shot from under Genghis Khan years earlier during the war against the Taijiut.

The 1218 victory over the Kara Khitai gave Genghis Khan control of the eastern part of the Silk Road. Caravans traveled the Silk Road carrying valuable trade goods between the Chinese in the east and the Muslims in the west. Genghis Khan learned much from the Muslim merchants who visited his court. He told his generals stationed along the Silk Road that they were to leave the population in peace. All people were allowed to practice their Muslim religion. Genghis Khan understood he could gain much by remaining on good terms with these merchant people.

FIGHTING THE KHWARIZM EMPIRE

TO THE WEST OF GENGHIS KHAN'S GROWING Mongol Empire was another great empire. The Khwarizm Empire stretched from the Pamir Mountains in the east to the Black Sea in the west. Its northern border touched the Aral Sea, and its southern border reached the Persian Gulf. The Khwarizm Empire included much of present-day Afghanistan, Iran, Kazakhstan, Pakistan, Turkmenistan, and Uzbekistan. Shah Muhammad II was the emperor of these conquered lands.

THE OTRAR MASSACRE

Genghis Khan wished to increase trade between the Mongol Empire and the Khwarizm Empire. In 1218, he sent ambassadors to the court of Shah Muhammad to offer a treaty. The Persian historian Juzjani reported that Genghis Khan told the shah: "I am master of the lands of the rising sun while you rule those of the setting sun. Let us conclude a firm treaty of friendship and peace."[1] He suggested that merchant caravans freely be allowed to travel back and forth. Shah Muhammad was unsure whether he should trust the Mongol ruler. But in the end, he agreed to the treaty.

Soon after their agreement, the Mongols sent a caravan westward led by four Muslim merchants. Four hundred fifty men drove five hundred richly loaded camels along the route.[2] On their backs, the camels carried bolts of Chinese silk, bars of silver, bundles of furs, and other valued trade goods.

At last, the caravan reached the Khwarizm border and entered the town of Otrar. The greedy governor of the region was a man named Inalchik. Inalchik seized the trade goods. His soldiers killed the four Muslim merchants and almost all of the camel drivers. Only one of the camel drivers managed to escape. He hurried eastward to report the news of the horrible massacre to Genghis Khan.

News of the Otrar massacre greatly angered Genghis Khan. He sent ambassadors to Shah Muhammad at his court in the Khwarizm city of Samarkand. The ambassadors included one Muslim, Ibn Khafraj Bughra, and two Mongols. Genghis Khan demanded the surrender of Inalchik for punishment for his crime. Instead, Shah Muhammad took the side of his governor. He had Ibn Khafraj Bughra beheaded. Then, as an added insult, he ordered that the two Mongol ambassadors have their beards shaved off. He sent them back to Mongolia in shame. This latest insult threw Genghis Khan into a rage. "The Khwarizm-shah is no king, he is a bandit!" he bitterly exclaimed.[3]

Genghis Khan returned to Burkhan Khaldun and climbed to the sacred mountaintop. There, he prayed for guidance. At the end of three days, he decided he must go to war against the Khwarizm Empire. The Mongols had already conquered Kara Khitai, which bordered on Khwarizm lands. His spies in that region swiftly gathered information about Khwarizm. Genghis Khan learned about the wealth of the towns, the strength of the Khwarizm army, and the weakness of Shah Muhammad's government. Genghis Khan called upon all Mongols to fight. He also gathered soldiers from the Uygurs, the Khitans, the Chinese, and other territories he ruled. He sent a request for troops to the Tangut king Li Xian, as well. Li Xian, however, refused to obey Genghis Khan's order. Genghis Khan vowed he would get revenge on the Tangut people someday. For the present, however, he must give all of his attention to the Khwarizm war.

In the summer of 1219, Genghis Khan gathered a huge army beside the Irtysh River. It numbered more than one hundred fifty thousand men. Almost all of these soldiers were cavalrymen. Only about ten thousand of them were Chinese siege engineers, especially trained in the methods of capturing walled cities.[4]

NAMING AN HEIR

Before marching off to war, Genghis Khan ordered that his youngest brother Temuge stay behind in Mongolia. It would be Temuge's duty to protect the homeland while Genghis Khan was away. Genghis Khan also called together another kuriltai. The Mongol ruler was fifty-six years old in 1218. He knew the war against the Khwarizm Empire would be difficult. One of his wives, the Tatar Yisui, had urged him to make plans for the future of the Mongol Empire. Genghis Khan realized he must choose one of the four sons of his first wife Borte to be great khan after his death.

Genghis Khan considered his choice carefully. He decided his oldest son, Jochi, was not skilled enough as a general. He did not have a high opinion of his second son, Chagatai, either. His third son, Ogodei, was very intelligent. But Ogodei often drank too much alcohol. His youngest son, Tolui, was a skilled and brave general. But Tolui was an even greater drunkard than Ogodei. In the end, Genghis Khan announced his choice. It was his wish that Ogodei should follow in his footsteps as great khan. His other sons promised to respect his decision.

During the kuriltai, Genghis Khan had many talks with his four sons. He gave them advice on how to be good rulers. Pride was one danger they needed to avoid. "If you can't swallow your pride," he warned them, "you can't lead."[5] He also told them always to have goals in life. "Without the vision of a goal," he stated, "a man cannot manage his own life, much less the lives of others."[6]

Genghis Khan divided his empire into kingdoms. Each area would be ruled by one of his sons or grandsons. But Ogodei would be great khan, leader of all. He would be the final judge of disagreements and be responsible for Mongol relations with foreign countries.

THE LONG MARCH WEST

Genghis Khan continued to gather and train his armies during the summer of 1219. By autumn, the Mongols were ready to march west toward the Syr Darya River. His spies in Khwarizm were already spreading stories to help the Mongol cause. They told of the fearsome bravery of Mongol soldiers. It would be hopeless, they warned, to resist them. The spies spread Genghis Khan's announcement that God had made him a gift of all the earth. Shah Muhammad had about four hundred thousand soldiers. But they were spread across his empire, defending many cities and towns. Genghis Khan believed he could conquer the Khwarizm Empire one city at a time.

In the late autumn of 1219, the Mongols at last reached the border town of Otrar. Chagatai and Ogodei were given command of the siege troops that surrounded Otrar. Genghis Khan, with his youngest son, Tolui, at his side, rode on to the southwest with the main Mongol army. Genghis Khan planned to capture the important city of Bukhara.

THE SEIGE OF BUKHARA

Genghis Khan and Tolui first rode with their horsemen across the Kizil Kum Desert. Along the way, the Mongols captured several small towns. The Persian historian Juzjani later wrote of the Mongol advance. When the people saw the countryside all around them "choked with horsemen and the air black as night with the dust of cavalry, fright and panic overcame them . . ."[7] Thousands of terrified people fled to Bukhara.

By February 1220, the Mongols reached Bukhara. Bukhara was a center of Muslim culture, a city full of schools and parks. The twelve thousand Khwarizm troops inside Bukhara defended the city for three days. Then they fought their way outside the city gates and tried to escape into the countryside. Most were slaughtered before they could get away. The following day, Bukhara surrendered.

Still, five hundred Khwarizm soldiers remained inside a fort, called the citadel, just outside the city. These men bravely held out for several more days. Forced to surrender at last, they were all put to death by Genghis Khan. When he at last entered Bukhara, he made an announcement to the frightened people. "I am the [scourge] of God," he told them. A scourge was a whip. "If you had not committed great sins," he continued, "God would not have sent a punishment like me upon you."[8]

Genghis Khan demanded the names of the city's richest people. He called them before him and declared, "What is still left in your houses you need not bother about, for we shall take care of that. Whatever you have hidden or

In this sixteenth-century illustration, Genghis Khan demands that Bukhara's richest citizens give him any valuables that they have hidden.

buried, you must bring to me."[9] These fearful Bukhara citizens quickly revealed where they had hidden their treasures. The Mongols looted Bukhara, taking everything they found of value. Soon, fire broke out and destroyed much of the city. The Mongols rounded up people and divided them into various groups. Skilled craftsmen were sent as slaves to Mongolia. Strong young men and women were forced to become the slaves of the army.

The treatment of the population of Bukhara was repeated in other Khwarizm towns. Sometimes, a town bravely resisted Mongol attack and caused the Mongols heavy losses. When such towns were finally captured, the Mongols massacred every enemy soldier they found. The skilled craftsmen, however, always were herded away with the women to be divided among the Mongols and made their slaves. After executing the soldiers, Mongol officers would send clerks into a town to divide the people by profession. Professional people included anyone who could read and write. Clerks, doctors, astronomers, judges, engineers, teachers, religious leaders were all spared. Merchants and skilled workers were useful to the Mongols, too. These included smiths, potters, carpenters, furniture makers, jewelers, and musicians.[10] People without skills were rounded up. The Mongols used them as workers. These slaves shoveled dirt, built ramps and siege towers, and served as human shields during attacks.

THE TERRIBLE MONGOLS

Medieval historians have recorded that Genghis Khan once declared, "The greatest joy a man can know is to conquer his enemies and drive them before him. To ride their horses and take away their possessions."[11] Genghis Khan understood the power of filling his enemies with fear. He was happy to have terrible stories spread about him and his soldiers. It did not matter whether they were true or not. The Arab writer Ibn al-Athir spread one story about the Mongols. "It is said," he described, "that a single one of them would enter a village [where there] were many people and would continue to slay them one after another . . ."[12]

In February 1220, Otrar was captured at last after a siege of five months. Toward the end of the siege, the governor Inalchik with twenty thousand troops fought from a fort inside the city. The battle to capture the fort lasted for many days. Most of the defenders died during the fighting. When the Khwarizm troops ran out of arrows, they threw roof tiles down on the attacking Mongols. Finally, Inalchik was captured and brought before Genghis Khan. According to the Muslim historian Nasawi, Genghis Khan had Inalchik killed in a gruesome way. Burning hot liquid silver was poured into Inalchik's eyes and ears.[13] A story such as this would certainly strike fear into the hearts of Mongol enemies.

THE SIEGE OF SAMARKAND

In March 1220, Genghis Khan left the smoking ruins of Bukhara behind. His next goal was Samarkand.

Samarkand (in present-day Uzbekistan) was a walled city with a population of half a million. It contained busy markets, great libraries, fabulous palaces, and a defending army of more than one hundred thousand men.[14] Genghis Khan's army approached Samarkand along both sides of the Zerafshan River. After surrounding the city, he had thousands of the prisoners who had been captured at Bukhara formed into regiments. The frightened people from within the city walls believed that they were surrounded by a huge army.

On the third day of the siege, more than fifty thousand of Samarkand's soldiers tried to fight their way out of the city. The Mongols slowly retreated before these massed troops. The Mongols found a good place from which to strike the enemy. When the moment arrived, they made a brutal counterattack. The Samarkand troops were slaughtered. On the fifth day, the last of the city's garrison hopelessly surrendered. The Mongols put them all to death.

The surviving people of Samarkand were divided into different groups. Skilled craftsmen were sent to Mongolia. All other young men were enslaved for the next siege. About three quarters of the people of Samarkand were either killed or made slaves.[15]

THE DEATH OF SHAH MUHAMMAD

Genghis Khan took the main part of the Mongol army across the mountains of Afghanistan as far as the Indus River. The city of Balkh surrendered without a fight.

Genghis Khan's policy of spreading terror was proving a success. The entire country had heard of what had happened in Samarkand.

Towns that surrendered were spared. Everyone who resisted was to be killed. Genghis Khan insisted that his Mongols obey his wishes. When Mongol troops commanded by his general Toguchar looted a town that had already surrendered, Genghis Khan punished him. He reduced Toguchar to the rank of a common cavalryman.

Genghis Khan rested his army until the autumn of 1220. Meanwhile, the tumens of his generals Jebei and Subodei chased after Shah Muhammad II. The loss of Samarkand had left Shah Muhammad in a desperate situation. Shah Muhammad fled from one place to another in search of safety. Jebei and Subodei hunted him across 2,000 miles of Khwarizm territory. In January 1221, Shah Muhammad landed on the little island of Abakan in the Caspian Sea. It was there that the defeated Khwarizm emperor died at last of pneumonia.

MONGOL RAIDERS

Jebei and Subodei with their army of twenty thousand horsemen had circled the Caspian Sea after chasing Shah Muhammad. After the shah's death, they asked Genghis Khan for permission to raid northward into the kingdom of Georgia and beyond. Genghis Khan gave them permission to raid the countryside.

In the autumn of 1221, Jebei and Subodei raided across northwestern Iran and spent the winter in Azerbaijan. In

Azerbaijan they were attacked by ten thousand cavalry, sent by George IV, king of Georgia. The Mongols destroyed this army and marched up the Kura River. At the city of Tiflis, they defeated a larger army sent from Georgia. One after another, the Mongol raiders defeated additional armies sent by the Kipchaks and the Bulgars. Queen Russudan of Georgia later wrote a letter to the Pope in Rome. "A savage people," she exclaimed, ". . . as brave as lions, have invaded my country."[16]

To the Dnieper River

Early in 1222, Mongol troops rode into the Crimean Peninsula on the north coast of the Black Sea. Here they successfully attacked and looted some Genoese trading posts. Genoese ships carried the news of the Mongol raiders to Italy.

The Mongols also swept across the Ukraine. In the spring of 1223, they learned that a Russian army of about eighty thousand soldiers was preparing to attack them. This army was commanded by Prince Mstislav of Galich. The Mongols made a long, nine-day withdrawal to the Kalka River. The Russians thought their enemy was fearfully retreating. The Russians rode after them until their horses were exhausted. Then the Mongols turned and suddenly struck. Riding into battle came the Russian advance guard of Kipchak horsemen. The Mongols let loose clouds of arrows. Many dead and wounded Kipchaks fell to the ground. When the battle ended, the entire Russian army was destroyed. A second Russian force arrived not long after. It was also destroyed. A third army, marching from the city of Kiev was surrounded by Mongol troops. In the fierce fight that followed, the Russians again met disaster. The Russians who survived fled in disorder all the way to the Dnieper River.

Jebei and Subodei celebrated their military successes with a drunken feast that lasted for days. The guests of honor were the captured Prince Mstislav of Kiev and his two sons-in-law. The Mongols rolled up the three noblemen in felt rugs. They lay them in the narrow space between the ground and the floorboards of their yurt. The Russian princes slowly smothered to death, as the Mongols drank and sang all night long in the yurt above them.[17]

The Mongol horsemen had raided as far west as the Dnieper River, north of the Black Sea. It was as far as they chose to go. In April 1223, near the present-day Russian city of Volgograd, they recrossed the Volga River heading eastward. Before the end of the year, Jebei and Subodei had rejoined Genghis Khan's army on the steppes east of the Syr Darya River.

JELAL AD-DIN

Before his death, Shah Muhammad II had named his son Jelal ad-Din to follow him on the Khwarizm throne. As the new shah, Jelal ad-Din retreated with the remains of the Khwarizm army into Afghanistan. By 1221, Jelal ad-Din was in Ghaznah, south of the Hindu Kush mountain region, raising additional troops. This is the region where the borders of Afghanistan, Pakistan, and India meet today. At Parwan, he succeeded in defeating a Mongol army commanded by Shigi Khutukhu. It was the first Mongol defeat of the entire war. Genghis Khan was embarrassed by Shigi Khutukhu's defeat. In his desire for revenge, he set out after Jelal ad-Din himself. Jelal ad-Din was forced to retreat to the Indus River with about fifty thousand soldiers.

In the autumn of 1221, near the city of Dinkot, the Mongols caught up with the Khwarizm army. Genghis Khan's horsemen attacked Jelal ad-Din's troops on the western side of the Indus River. Unable to cross the river in time, Jelal ad-Din's army was trapped. In the battle that followed, the Khwarizm army was destroyed. At the end of the fight, Jelal ad-Din made one last charge with the last seven hundred men of his bodyguard. He snatched a Khwarizm flag that the Mongols had captured. Spurring his horse, he galloped away in an attempt to escape. When Jelal ad-Din and his horse reached the low cliffs beside the river, they made a daring leap outwards and splashed into the water far below. Jelal ad-Din managed to escape across the river.

Genghis Khan watched this bold escape in amazement. "One cannot believe," he exclaimed, "that such a father could have produced such a son!"[18] Jelal ad-Din retreated into India. Behind him, the Khwarizm Empire lay in ruins. But Jelal ad-Din would continue to fight until 1231, when he was finally murdered.

THE SURRENDER OF GURGANJ

Jelal ad-Din's refusal to surrender to the Mongols sparked revolts in such Khwarizm cities as Herat, Merv, and Balkh. The Mongols had to recapture those cities after difficult sieges. It was claimed that more than a million people were slaughtered by the Mongols while recapturing Merv. The city of Balkh was also totally destroyed. It was reported the Mongols left no creature alive in Balkh other than a few barking dogs.[19]

In order to capture the city of Gurganj, Genghis Khan called for troops commanded by his sons Chagatai and Ogodei to join forces with his oldest son Jochi. Gurganj was partly surrounded by marshland. There were no large stones to be found. As a result, the Mongols cut down trees. Their catapults threw large chunks of wood instead of stones at the city walls. When the Mongols finally broke into the city, the people of Gurganj bravely defended themselves. Both sides suffered many deaths. The Mongols struggled ahead through one section of the city after another. Fires broke out, and at last, the beaten defenders begged for mercy and surrendered in April 1221.

Mongol soldiers began to loot Gurganj. It is uncertain how it happened, but the dike along the Amu Darya River soon burst. A dike is a wall of dirt built to hold back water. Much of Gurganj flooded, and many citizens drowned. Genghis Khan had made a promise to his son Jochi. Jochi would rule the entire region when the war ended. After the capture of Gurganj, Jochi stayed to rule all of the territory around the Aral Sea.

HORROR AT NISHAPUR

After recapturing the city of Nissa, the Mongols tied up seventy thousand people. The Mongols killed these people as they stood completely defenseless. Other slaughters followed. One of the most terrible was suffered by the citizens of Nishapur. Genghis Khan had warned these people, "Whoever submits shall be spared, but those who resist, they shall be destroyed."[20] The people of Nishapur at first surrendered. However, many of the citizens soon regretted that decision and chose to rebel and defend themselves. In the siege that followed, an arrow struck and killed Genghis Khan's son-in-law Titjar.

Nishapur held out for three days. The Mongol army possessed hundreds of catapults which sent huge rocks crashing into the city walls. At last in April 1221, the Mongols finally broke into the city. When he finally captured Nishapur, Genghis Khan allowed his daughter, wife of the killed Titjar, to decide the fate of the citizens. She demanded death for all of them. Mongol soldiers carried out her grim orders. According to stories, she ordered the soldiers to heap the heads of the dead citizens in three separate piles. There were piles for the men, the women, and the children. Then it was reported she ordered that all of the dogs, cats, and other living animals in the city also be slaughtered. She wished the complete ruin of Nishapur as revenge for the death of her husband.[21]

OMAR KHAYYAM OF NISHAPUR

One hundred years before the Mongols destroyed Nishapur, a man named Omar Khayyam lived in the Persian city. Omar Khayyam is best remembered as a poet. He wrote some seven hundred fifty "quatrains," or four-line verses of poetry. Collected together, these short poems are known as *The Rubaiyat*. The verses describe such things as the beauty of nature and the joys of love:

> A Book of Verses underneath the Bough,
> A Jug of Wine, a Loaf of Bread—and Thou
> Beside me singing in the Wilderness—
> Oh, Wilderness were Paradise enow![22]

BAMIYAN

In the beautiful valley of Bamiyan in Afghanistan, the Mongols needed to recapture another rebellious town. During the siege at Bamiyan, an arrow struck and killed Genghis Khan's favorite grandson, Mutugen. Genghis Khan was deeply saddened and greatly enraged by the death. When the town was finally captured, he ordered his troops to kill every living thing they found.

Mutugen had been Chagatai's son. Chagatai soon reached the Mongol camp outside the destroyed city. Genghis Khan sternly demanded if his son would obey anything he commanded. Chagatai dropped to his knees. He solemnly swore that he would obey. "Your son is dead," Genghis Khan then revealed. "I forbid you to weep and complain."[23] Chagatai carried out his oath. He never wept or complained about the death of his son.

Governing an Empire

Genghis Khan led his army at last into the mountains of the Hindu Kush. There, he established his winter camp. He sent Mongol troops forward, and they captured the cities of Multan and Lahore (in present-day Pakistan). The Mongols continued to advance into India. In the summer of 1222, the heat of the Punjab plains of India, however, forced the Mongols to withdraw again into the mountains.

After four years of war, Genghis Khan had conquered the Khwarizm Empire. In 1222, the Year of the Horse, Genghis Khan called for an end to Mongol fighting. For a time, Genghis Khan had thought of conquering all of northern India. His plan would have included marching across the Himalayan Mountains and into southern China. He soon realized, however, that the high mountains, thick forests, and hot climate of India made his plan nearly impossible. As a result, he decided to march back to Mongolia by the same route by which he had come.

Great Khwarizm cities now lay in smoking ruins. Never before, not in Mongolia or in China, had Genghis Khan's Mongol troops caused so much death and ruin. Genghis Khan made arrangements for the governing of the conquered Khwarizm lands. He appointed personal governors called *darughachi* to rule each of the major cities. It was their duty to collect taxes, recruit troops, organize the messenger service, and send reports to Mongolia. Then, at the age of sixty, Genghis Khan began his plans for marching homeward.

THE WORLD CONQUEROR

ONE OF GENGHIS KHAN'S LAWS DEMANDED, "When the Mongols are unoccupied by war, they shall devote themselves to hunting."[1] Before leaving the Khwarizm Empire, Genghis Khan called for a celebration. During the winter of 1222–1223, soldiers roped off a large area of land with long pieces of horsehair twine. The roped area formed a great circle, many miles round. Genghis Khan wished to celebrate his victory by holding a great hunt. These great hunts, or *abas* as the Mongols called them, were partly to supply the army with meat. They also served as an important military practice.

THE GREAT HUNT

When all was ready, the hunt began at the outer edge of the great circle. Soldiers beat drums and banged cymbals together. Slowly they walked forward. The circle grew smaller and smaller with each step they took. Every thicket, piece of marshland, and cave was to be searched. No wild beast of any kind was to be allowed to escape.

Slowly and surely, the animals inside the shrinking circle were driven back. Only when the beasts had been herded into an inner circle could the killing begin. Thousands of soldiers took part in the hunt that followed. By then, the enraged wild animals they faced were as ferocious as any human enemy they might meet in war. The hunters killed all kinds of animals: tigers, bears, leopards, wild boars, herds of antelopes, rabbits, and birds. The hunt, through forests and across streams, sharpened their skills both as horsemen and as military planners. The aba gave the men practice with their weapons. It strengthened them in mind and body. Altogether, the great hunt lasted about four months.

GENGHIS KHAN AND THE WISE MAN

Back in 1219, Genghis Khan had been gathering his army on the Kara Irtysh River for the war against the Khwarizm Empire. It was there that he had learned of a Chinese wise man named Chang Chun. He asked Chang Chun to travel from the Chinese province of Shandong and visit him.

"I am old . . . and fear I shall be unable to endure the pains of such a long journey," Chang Chun wrote to Genghis Khan.[2] Still, Genghis Khan demanded to see him. The aged Chinese scholar Chang Chun finally reached Genghis Khan's camp in the southern Hindu Kush during the spring of 1222.

Genghis Khan was no longer a young man. His health had suffered from the many hardships of march and battle. He happily welcomed Chang Chun into his royal yurt. He gave him a seat near him and ordered food to be served. He believed Chang Chun possessed medical secrets. He asked the wise man, "What medicine of long life have you brought me from afar?"[3] Chang Chun plainly answered that there was no such medicine.

Genghis Khan did not show his disappointment. Instead, he thanked Chang Chun for his honesty. He treated the wise old man with honor and kindness. During Chang Chun's long visit, the two men talked together several times. Genghis Khan listened respectfully to Chang Chun's teachings and ordered that his words of wisdom be written down.

THE LONG JOURNEY HOME

In the autumn of 1222, Genghis Khan and his Mongol horsemen at last began the long journey homeward. In the winter of 1222–1223, they rested in the region of Samarkand. In the spring of 1223, Genghis Khan's sons Chagatai, Ogodei, and Tolui rejoined him. Jochi had chosen to stay behind in his kingdom between the Aral Sea and the Caspian Sea. As a gift to his father, Jochi sent twenty thousand spotted horses. Subodei also rejoined his great khan. He brought wonderful tales of his raid into the West. He also sadly reported that Jebei had died of a fever.

During 1224, the Mongol army moved eastward to the Irtysch River. From there, the march continued toward

Mongolia. The Mongol advance included carts packed with looted treasure, great herds of horses and cattle, and thousands of slaves.

Genghis Khan at last reached the border of Mongolia in the spring of 1225. Among the first Mongols he met were his two youngest grandsons. Hulegu was eleven years old and Kublai was nine years old. They were sons of Tolui. The two boys had successfully finished their first hunt when Genghis Khan came upon them. Following an old custom, Genghis Khan rubbed their thumbs with the blood of the deer and the rabbit that they had killed. By doing so, it was hoped the two boys would always be lucky hunters.

WAR AGAINST THE TANGUTS

The medieval Chinese historian Yuen-chao-pi-shi wrote that Genghis Khan had an unusual habit during the Khwarizm war. Twice each day, he had himself reminded that the Tangut kingdom of Xi-Xia had not yet been destroyed. He wanted always to remember the oath he had sworn before marching off to fight Shah Muhammad.[4] Genghis Khan had not forgotten the rebellious Tanguts while he was in the West. The Tanguts had refused to send him troops for his war against the Khwarizm Empire. Instead, the Tanguts had risen in open rebellion against Mongol rule. In 1226, Genghis Khan rode out at the head of his army to put down the Tangut rebellion.

That winter, while crossing the Gobi Desert, Genghis Khan stopped to hunt wild horses. During the hunt, he

The Great Khan and his Mongol warriors storm a Tangut
fortress in this sixteenth-century Persian illustration.

took a rough fall from his horse. He may have suffered internal injuries as a result of his fall. In spite of this, however, he continued onward with his army. The Mongols crossed the Gobi Desert and made a surprise attack upon the Tanguts. The cities of Suzhou and Ganzhou were captured after sieges. In September 1226, Genghis Khan attacked General Ashagambu's Tangut army beside the Yellow River. In the cold weather, the plain beside the river had become a frozen sheet of ice. The Mongols wrapped their horses' hooves with cloth to keep them from slipping. Genghis Khan sent his best archers on foot to attack across the plain. The Tangut cavalry charged forward. Many of the Tangut horses slid and fell on the ice. The Mongol archers made a sudden charge on the helpless riders from all sides. Then, quickly mounting their own horses, the Mongols cut down advancing Tangut infantry. The Tanguts scattered in defeat.

By February 1227, the Mongol army had reached the Tangut city Ningxia. The injuries Genghis Khan had suffered from his horse fall continued to bother him. By now, he suffered from a high fever. His Mongol generals suggested that he break off the campaign. They advised that he return home and get proper medical attention. Genghis Khan refused to consider this advice. "If we go," he declared, "the Tanguts will certainly think I was afraid of them."[5]

By August 1227, food supplies inside Ningxia ran out. The Tangut king, Li Xian, was forced to surrender. He only asked that Genghis Khan grant a month's truce so that he could prepare gifts for his conqueror.

DEATH OF THE GREAT KHAN

In the Mongol camp outside Ningxia, Genghis Khan's great yurt was easy to recognize. In front of the royal tent stood a lance with its point in the ground. This was the Mongol way of announcing that the yurt's owner lay sick.[6] Genghis Khan guessed that he was dying. He had recently learned that his oldest son Jochi had died in his faraway kingdom. Now, as he lay on his bed, Genghis Khan gathered his other sons and grandsons around him.

"With Heaven's aid I have conquered for you a huge empire," he told them. "From the middle of it a man may ride for a year eastward or westward without reaching its limits. But my life was too short to achieve the conquest of the world. That task is left for you. Be of one mind and one faith, that you may conquer your enemies and lead long and happy lives."[7]

He urged his family to remain always loyal to one another. He asked each of them to break a single arrow. This they all could easily do. Then he had them each try to break several arrows bound together. This none of them could do. According to *The Secret History*, he told them, "You will be as firm as that if you all hold together. Believe nobody, never trust an enemy, help and support each other in life's dangers, obey my laws . . . and carry every action you begin to its conclusion."[8]

On a day in August 1227, Genghis Khan died at last. He was sixty-five years old. He had ordered that his death be kept secret until after the surrender of Ningxia. When the Tangut king Li Xian presented himself in September, he bowed low before the entrance of the royal yurt. He was not told that Genghis Khan lay dead inside. Three days later, the Tangut king and all of his family were executed. Nearly the entire population of the city was also put to death. The Mongols looted Ningxia and destroyed many of its buildings. Genghis Khan had kept his promise. The Tangut nation had been conquered and punished for its rebellion.

THE LAST JOURNEY

Genghis Khan's Tatar wife Yisui prepared his body for burial. Servants cleaned the body and dressed it in a plain white robe. Felt boots were put on his feet and a handsome hat on his head. Then the body was wrapped in a white felt blanket along with bits of lovely smelling sandalwood. The felt coffin was bound together with three golden straps. At last, the funeral procession started northward toward Mongolia. The Great Khan's body was carried on a simple cart.

Genghis Khan had ordered that his death be kept a complete secret. As a result, whenever the funeral procession met with people, they were killed. At the end of the long journey, the body was wheeled up the steep, wooded slopes of Burkhan Khaldun. Near the mountaintop stood a single tree. Years earlier, while hunting, Genghis Khan once had rested under the tree. He had gazed about him and said, "This is a good place for me to be buried. Take note of it."[9]

Beneath this tree, Genghis Khan was buried, along with the royal cart that had brought him there. The location was kept secret. After filling in the grave, eight hundred horsemen rode back and forth over the area to stamp out any trace of its location. For years, a guard of Urianghai horsemen protected the place and kept people away. Today, the exact spot where Genghis Khan is buried remains unknown. With the death and burial of Genghis Khan, his rule had come to an end. The rule of the Mongol Empire, however, would last for many more years.

Mongol Invaders

GENGHIS KHAN WAS DEAD. A NEW KHAN NEEDED to be chosen. His son Tolui, as khan of the Mongol steppes, called for a kuriltai of Mongol leaders. In the autumn of 1229, the Mongol chiefs gathered near the headwaters of the Kerulen River. At this meeting, they named Ogodei the new ruler of the Mongol Empire. This had been the wish of Genghis Khan.

Ogodei Becomes Great Khan

Ogodei chose to build a capital city west of the Mongol steppe. He built the city of Karakorum beside the Orkhon River, on lands that had belonged to the Naiman. There were two business sections in Karakorum. The Muslim section contained the city's markets. Merchants crowded the streets, buying and selling goods. The city's other business area was Chinese. Here, Chinese craftsmen made objects of value, such as furniture and jewelry, for sale.

Ogodei was a calm, careful, and wise ruler. During his years as great khan, he improved the mounted messenger service. He also had wells dug to make life easier for his people. To improve trade, Ogodei developed a standardized system of weights and measures. Some Mongols also began using paper money. This made trade much easier. During Ogodei's rule, the Mongols planted trees beside their roads. These trees provided travelers with welcome shade from the hot sun.

THE SILVER TREE

Ogodei had several large palaces built at Karakorum. His secretaries worked in these, keeping records of the empire. At the entrance of Ogodei's own great palace stood an amazing tree made of silver. It had been built by a craftsman named Master Guillaume of Paris, a captured slave. At the foot of the silver tree were four silver lions. White mare's milk poured out of each lion's mouth from tubes Master Guillaume had designed. Four pipes inside the tree rose all the way to the tree top and then down again. From these pipes flowed liquids that poured out of the mouths of four golden serpents, or snakes. One pipe flowed with wine, another with kumiss. A third poured out boal, a drink made of honey. The fourth pipe let drinkers fill their cups with rice beer. Visitors to the royal palace at Karakorum marveled at this fantastic silver tree.

THE TARTAR HORDES

While Ogodei served as great khan, Mongol wars of conquest continued. By 1234, the last of the Jin Empire in northern China had been conquered. During the next six years, the independent kingdom of Korea was also brought under Mongol control.

The Mongols had not forgotten the successful raid in the West made by Jebei and Subodei. During a kuriltai in 1235, it was decided to send a large army to conquer thousands of square miles of steppes north of the Aral and Caspian seas. These were the lands of the Kipchak and Bulgar people. Even farther west, north of the Black Sea, was the territory of the Russians.

The command of the Mongol invasion army was given to Batu, Jochi's second son. He would be guided by the general Subodei. The Mongols gathered an army of about fifty thousand horsemen. Another one hundred thousand cavalrymen from conquered Turkish territory also joined the march.

In 1236, the main army set out. In time, they reached the Volga River. Subodei led one army northward into Bulgar territory. Tolui's son, Mongke, led another army south against the Kipchaks. In 1237, Subodei's army smashed the Bulgars and sent them fleeing. At the same time, Mongke attacked the Kipchaks along the lower Volga River. Batu's combined armies swiftly conquered both the Kipchaks and the Bulgars.

In December 1237, the Mongols marched northward into Russia. During the winter of 1237–1238 the invaders captured Rostov, Moscow, and other Russian towns. Many Europeans called the Mongols "Tartars." Some Mongols, after all, had been members of the Tatar tribe. The name Tartar was similar to the classical name Tartarus, which was thought to be a region of Hell. To many Europeans, the Mongols seemed to be devils on earth, so it was natural for the name Tartar to become attached to the hated Mongols.[1] In 1238, the Mongols attacked the Russian city of Riazan. In *The Chronicle of Novgorod*, a Russian historical journal, it was noted that "Tartars came in countless numbers, like locusts."[2] Locusts are a kind of grasshopper. They travel in great swarms and will swoop down on a field and eat everything in sight. After a siege at Riazan, the Mongols rode into the city. The feared horsemen rounded up all of the city's nobles and killed them. A Russian writer sadly exclaimed that after the Mongol army left "no eye remained open to cry for the dead."[3]

THE CAPTURE OF KIEV

In the spring of 1240, Batu's armies pushed farther westward. Soon they surrounded the city of Kiev on the Dnieper River. Kiev was the most important city in the Ukraine. The soldiers stationed in Kiev defended themselves against the Mongols. A witness named Dmitri wrote of the Mongol attack: "They broke through the city walls and entered the city. . . . One could see and hear a great clash of lances and clatter of shields." So many arrows were shot into the air, Dmitri declared, "that it became impossible to see the sky. . . . there were dead everywhere."[4] Kiev fell to the invaders on December 6, 1240. The Mongol forces looted Kiev and burned it to the ground. A traveler passing through the city more than twenty years later was shocked. He saw only two hundred houses left standing in Kiev. Outside the ruined town, the bones of the dead still lay unburied.

With the fall of Kiev, thousands of Russians fled into eastern Europe. Close behind them rode the feared Mongol horsemen. In 1240, an English monk named Matthew Paris remarked that the Mongols invaded Russia "with the force of lightning . . . committing great slaughter, and striking . . . terror and alarm into every one."[5]

THE BATTLE OF LIEGNITZ

The capture of Kiev left the path into eastern Europe completely open. Subodei sent three army columns totaling fifty thousand soldiers toward Hungary. At the same time, another Mongol column of twenty thousand horsemen rode toward Poland in the north. This smaller force was meant to keep Polish and German enemies busy while Hungary was being attacked.

In February 1241, the smaller Mongol force entered Poland. One Polish city after another was taken, as the Mongols galloped across the plains. Duke Henry II of the kingdom of Silesia gathered an army of thirty thousand soldiers to defend western Poland. Riding among these troops were knights from Germany, France, and Poland. On April 9, 1241, the Mongols clashed with these soldiers near the city of Liegnitz.

During the bloody fight, the Mongol horsemen pretended to retreat, as they did so often in battle. Duke Henry's knights galloped after them, until their horses were exhausted. Suddenly, the Mongols turned and struck. Mongol arrows whizzed through the air and hit their targets. Thousands of dead and wounded knights dropped from their horses. The Mongols won a complete victory at Liegnitz.

THE PLAIN OF MOHI

The success of the Mongols in Poland allowed Subodei's larger army to advance easily across the plains of Hungary. The Mongols looted town after town, as they rode westward toward the Danube River. King Bela of Hungary raised an army to defend his homeland. When the Hungarian army advanced at last, the Mongols fell back. They rode eastward for several days. Subodei waited until King Bela's army made camp on the plain of Mohi. On April 11, 1241, the Mongols swiftly surrounded the Hungarian position.

After surrounding the enemy, the Mongols opened a gap. They allowed the Hungarian army to retreat toward the city of Pest (the eastern half of present-day Budapest). As the Hungarians fled, their panic grew. The medieval historian Thomas of Spalato later called the Mongols "de Peste Tartorum," meaning "The Tartar Plague." Spalato described the slaughter of the Hungarians as they retreated. The dead, he exclaimed, "fell to the right and left like leaves of winter."[6] The French Archbishop of

125

Bordeaux received a report that the Mongols were "cannibals from Hell who eat the dead after a battle and leave only bones . . ."[7] There is, however, no real evidence that the Mongols ever ate human flesh. Five days after the battle, the Mongols captured Pest on the Danube River. They looted the city and then set it on fire. Mongol soldiers chased after King Bela as far as the island of Tran in the Adriatic Sea.

By the summer of 1241, all of eastern Europe from the Baltic Sea to the Danube River had been raided by the Mongols. Much of present-day Moldova, Belarus, Lithuania, Romania, and Poland had been overrun. By December 1241, Mongol scouts had ridden to the very gates of Vienna, Austria. Throughout the winter, the Mongols remained in Hungary. Then, in 1242, the Mongols suddenly headed eastward. A messenger had traveled thousands of miles from Karakorum and had brought Batu the news that Ogodei had died on December 11, 1241. He had died of the effects of his heavy drinking.

Ogodei's death saved western Europe from Mongol invasion. Batu knew he must immediately return to Mongolia. A kuriltai was gathering for the election of a new great khan. After seven years away from home, Batu's Mongol army began the long march back to Mongolia.

Chagatai had died at about the same time as Ogodei. Tolui had died sometime earlier. As a result, just fourteen years after the death of Genghis Khan, all four of his sons were dead. Now, it would be up to Genghis Khan's grandsons to hold the Mongol Empire together.

GIOVANNI DE PLANO CARPINI

In 1246, Toregene, Ogodei's widow, arranged for her son Guyuk to be elected the next great khan. At the election kuriltai, in July 1246, the first ambassador from western Europe arrived at the Mongol court. Giovanni de Plano Carpini was a sixty-five-year-old friar of the Roman Catholic Church. He had journeyed all the way from Europe carrying letters from Pope Innocent IV. The Pope hoped to improve diplomatic relations with the Mongols. The Mongols received Carpini with courtesy and allowed him to move through their camp freely.

During his visit to Mongolia, Carpini learned much about Mongol culture. Not everything he claimed was absolutely true. He reported things as he saw them. "As soon as the children are two or three years old," Carpini wrote, "they begin to ride. . . . and then a small bow . . . is given to them and they are taught to shoot."[8] Perhaps the children he observed were not quite so young. Being small, they seemed very young to Carpini.

Carpini noticed that the weather on the Mongolian steppes was unusual. He described:

> In the middle of summer, when other places are normally enjoying very great heat, there is fierce thunder and lightning which cause the death of many men, and at the same time there are very heavy falls of snow. There are also hurricanes of bitterly cold wind so violent that at times men can ride on horseback only with great effort.[9]

Carpini also took note of Mongolian eating habits. "They have neither bread nor herbs nor vegetables nor anything else, nothing but meat," reported Carpini, "of which, however, they eat so little that other people would scarcely be able to exist on it . . . They do not use table cloths or napkins," he further remarked. ". . . They make their hands very dirty with the grease of the meat, but when they eat they wipe them on . . . the grass or some other such thing. . . . They do not wash their dishes . . ."[10] Carpini successfully returned to Europe in 1247. He published a book about his many adventures. It was called *Description of the Mongols Whom We Call Tartars.*

HULEGU KHAN

Guyuk died after serving only a year and a half as great khan. Another kuriltai in the summer of 1251 declared Tolui's son Mongke great khan. During his eight years as leader, Mongke spread Mongol rule farther east and west. He sent his brother Hulegu west to attack the Middle East. Another brother, Kublai, was sent south to conquer the Song Empire in southern China. In May 1253, Hulegu and Kublai left Mongolia on their military campaigns.

A Muslim religious group called Ismaili controlled much of the territory stretching from Afghanistan to Syria. Some members of the Ismaili went by the name Assassins. Today the word "assassin" has entered the English language as the name for any political killer. Hulegu's Mongol army marched into the region and battled the Assassins. By November 19, 1256, the Mongols had beaten these enemies.

After conquering the Assassins, Hulegu's army marched on toward Baghdad (the present-day capital of Iraq). Baghdad was the greatest of all Muslim cities. By the start of 1258, the Mongols set up camps circling the city. The medieval Persian historian Wassaf noted, "In this way Baghdad was besieged and terrorized for fifty days."[11] In February, the Mongols broke through the city walls and Baghdad fell into their hands. The Mongols rolled the caliph, ruler of the city, into a carpet. Then the Mongols trampled him to death with their horses.

From Baghdad, the Mongols rode farther west toward the city of Damascus (in present-day Syria). The people of Damascus greatly feared the approaching Mongols. They had heard stories of terrible Mongol behavior. The city surrendered without a fight. All of Syria swiftly fell under Mongol control. Before long, Mongol warriors had reached the coast of the Mediterranean Sea. They had scored a most remarkable success. In their long war to recapture the Holy Land, European crusaders had only managed to capture a few Mediterranean seacoast cities. In much less time, the Mongols had conquered thousands of miles of Muslim territory from the Indus River to the Mediterranean Sea.

Hulegu now turned his attention to the kingdom of Egypt. In 1259, his army marched toward the Nile River. In that year, however, Mongke died. After learning of the great khan's death, Hulegu left the Middle East. He journeyed home to attend the next election kuriltai in Mongolia.

A DIVIDED EMPIRE

While Hulegu had been conquering the Muslims in the West, his brother Kublai had been fighting in southern China. Kublai's army fought many battles, but he was less successful than Hulegu. In May 1258, Mongke Khan arrived in China to take personal command of the Mongol army there. When he suddenly died on August 11, 1259, the future of the Mongol Empire became uncertain. Mongke Khan would be the last Mongol to be accepted as Great Khan by the entire Mongol Empire.

The Mongol Empire had become subdivided into four huge kingdoms ruled by members of Genghis Khan's family. One branch of the family came to be called The Golden Horde. The Golden Horde ruled countries stretching from eastern Europe to Kazakhstan and western Siberia. The branch of the family headed by Hulegu ruled the lands stretching from Afghanistan to Turkey. This kingdom became known as the Ilkhanate. The most traditional Mongols still lived on the central Asian steppes. This area included lands stretching from eastern Kazakhstan and Siberia in the north to Turkistan and Afghanistan in the south. The fourth region was ruled by Genghis Khan's grandson Kublai. It included China, Tibet, Korea, and eastern Mongolia.

KUBLAI KHAN

In 1262, Mongol chieftains chose Kublai to be their leader. Even though Kublai was called Great Khan, he never enjoyed the complete control over the Mongol people that Genghis Khan did. Rulers of the Ilkhanate and the Golden Horde both recognized his authority but acted independently from him. These branches of the family had adopted the religions and customs of their kingdoms. Mongol traditions and laws were no longer considered important to them.

Kublai Khan established his capital at Shangdu in China. Carefully and wisely, Kublai Khan used ambassadors to bring the Song Empire in southern China under Mongol rule. While khan, Kublai expanded the arrow messenger service throughout China. It is believed as many as two hundred thousand horses were used to deliver messages.[12] He also ordered that granaries be built. Wheat and other grains could be stored in these buildings until they were needed. Chinese laborers constructed hospitals at his command in order to care for the sick and injured. Workers also built schools, so children could be educated. Thousands of miles of roads and bridges were kept in good condition and patrolled by soldiers. This made travel safe and easy throughout his empire.

While keeping Shangdu as a summer home, in 1272, Kublai Khan ordered a city built to the south on the ruins of Zhongdu. It would be his new capital. Workers dug a canal so that the city was connected by water to the Yellow River. The Chinese subjects called the new capital Dadu. The Mongols called the new capital Khanbalik, meaning the "City of the Khan."[13] Inside Dadu, Kublai built a grand palace surrounded by parkland, which became called The Forbidden City. In time, Dadu would grow in size.

Today it is the city of Beijing in the People's Republic of China.

MARCO POLO

In 1275, three merchants arrived at the court of Kublai Khan. They were twenty-year-old Marco Polo and his father and uncle. The three men had traveled thousands of miles from the city of Venice in Italy. Marco Polo has given us a description of Kublai Khan: "He is neither short nor tall but of [middle] height," Marco Polo wrote. ". . . His complexion is fair and ruddy like a rose, the eyes are black and handsome, the nose shapely and set squarely in place."[14] Marco Polo also described Kublai Khan's great palace. "The palace . . . has a very high roof," he revealed. "Inside, the walls of the halls and chambers are all covered with gold and silver and decorated with pictures of dragons and birds and horsemen and various . . . beasts and scenes of battles."[15]

Kublai Khan was impressed by Marco Polo's intelligence. He soon appointed the young man as an imperial ambassador. During the next seventeen years, Marco Polo traveled throughout the empire in service to the great khan. In the course of his journeys, Marco Polo saw many things no European had ever seen before. In Europe, only gold, silver, and copper coins were used as money. But in China, paper money was used. Marco Polo explained that it was made "out of the bark of trees . . . from mulberry trees."[16] He also described a remarkable fuel that was used for heat. "There is a sort of black stone," he explained,

Kublai Khan made a cultural connection to Europe when he received Marco Polo and gave him gifts and a position in his government.

"which is dug out of . . . the hillsides and burns like logs. These stones keep a fire going better than wood."[17] With this description, many Europeans learned for the first time about coal.

In 1292, Marco Polo, along with his father and uncle, left China. They made the long, hard journey all the way back to Venice. Marco Polo later wrote a book, telling of his travels in Asia. Readers are still amazed today to learn about the things he saw while serving Kublai Khan.

The Kamikaze

The islands of Japan to the east of China attracted the interest of Kublai Khan. In November 1274, he sent ten thousand Korean and Chinese soldiers across the sea. They landed on the southern Japanese island of Kyushu. These soldiers might have conquered all of Japan. But a sudden storm forced them to retreat back to the mainland of Asia. The Japanese named the terrific storm that saved them the "Kamikaze," meaning "The Divine Wind." They believed the wind had been sent by God.

In 1281, Kublai decided to invade Japan again. Aboard three thousand five hundred ships, an army of one hundred thousand men set sail.[18] The second invasion of Japan was a failure. Kublai Khan's army was defeated by a Japanese army. Before it could reorganize, the great fleet anchored on the coast of Japan was struck by another mighty storm. The invasion ships were tossed about like toys. Many boats smashed together or tipped over and sank. The damaged ships struggled back to Asia. Surviving

soldiers were grateful to be alive. Again, the Japanese had
been saved by the Kamikaze.

END OF THE EMPIRE

While he was great khan, Kublai continued to send armies
southward across Asia. His soldiers defeated many enemies
and conquered many lands, including parts of present-day
Thailand, Myanmar, Vietnam, and Malaysia. The great
khan's troops even crossed the water, in order to invade the
Indonesian island of Java and the Philippine Islands.

In 1294, after ruling for thirty-four years, Kublai Khan
died. By then, the Mongol Empire was no longer as
powerful as it had once been. Genghis Khan's family
continued to grow apart. The distances among the several
kingdoms were too far. The differences in religions and
customs among the people of Asia were too great.

In addition, a deadly disease helped break up the
Mongol Empire. Bubonic plague, or the Black Plague, was
a deadly disease that lived in fleas. The fleas spread far and
wide, traveling on the backs of rats. By 1351, it is believed
more than half of the population of China had died of
Bubonic plague.[19] Fear of the plague stopped trade and
communications across all of Asia. The great empire built
by Genghis Khan gradually collapsed. In China, the rule of
the Mongols was finally overthrown when the Chinese
Ming dynasty took power in 1368.

THE BLACK PLAGUE

The Bubonic plague, or Black Plague, first appeared in Mongol-ruled China in 1313. The deadly disease quickly spread across Asia and Europe. Fleas and flea-infested rats carried the disease westward on trade ships and merchant caravans. By 1348, people as far away as in London, England, were dropping dead in the streets of the terrible Black Plague.[20]

MONGOL GIFTS TO THE WORLD

During the height of the Mongol Empire, many things happened to help the advance of civilization. The safety of trade routes across all of Asia allowed the easy exchange of goods and information, new inventions, and ideas. Merchant caravans carried many valued products westward for Europeans to buy and enjoy. A smooth and shiny type of silk became known in Europe as satin, for example, because it came from the Mongol port of Zaytun. Another type of cloth became known as damask silk, because it traveled through the city of Damascus on its journey west. A fine cloth made in the city of Mosul (in present-day Iraq) is known in English today as muslin cloth.

The Mongols used felt carpets to cover the dirt floors of their yurts. They also used woven carpets after conquering Persia and Turkestan where such beautiful carpets were made. The use of felt and woven carpets spread wherever the Mongols traveled. Agriculture also changed as Mongol influence grew. Crops grown in China

This modern-day Mongolian family lives in the area where Genghis Khan was from. The man in the foreground is making felt. In the background is the family's yurt.

such as tea and rice were carried westward by the Mongols into Persia and the Middle East. Farmers in China began to plant lemon trees and carrots, which were first Persian crops. Other foods such as peas, beans, grapes, nuts, turnips, and melons all traveled either eastward or westward. Chinese noodles also became popular in new lands as the Mongols carried them westward.

The Mongols brought more than just death and destruction with them on their many marches westward. For fun, Mongol soldiers sometimes played a game on horseback. They hit a wooden ball toward a goal with mallets. Today, the Mongol game of polo is still played throughout the world. Another activity Mongol soldiers enjoyed during idle hours became even more popular as it traveled worldwide. It was the Mongols who spread the use of playing cards.

The Mongols spread many important and practical inventions, too. It was Mongol cavalrymen who first used leather stirrups attached to their saddles. Stirrups gave riders better balance and skill in horsemanship. Wandering horsemen had spread this valuable invention westward many years before the rise of Genghis Khan. The Chinese inventions of printing, gunpowder, and the compass, however, all spread westward during the days of the Mongol Empire.

Even some Mongol words have entered the English language. The Mongol word for camp is *ordu*. As swarms of Mongol horsemen threatened the West, they became known as "hordes." The word horde today refers to any great crowd. It is possible that a Mongol war cry is even better known to English speakers today. People loudly shout "hurray" when they want to cheer. It is believed by at least one scholar that the Mongols shouted the same word before charging into battle.[21]

THE LEGEND OF GENGHIS KHAN

When Genghis Khan died in 1227, he was the ruler of the largest empire ever created by one person. No one else in history won as many battles, captured as many cities, or conquered as many kingdoms. Genghis Khan's Mongol Empire stretched from the Pacific Ocean to the Black Sea. The territory he conquered included thirty modern

MODERN MONGOLIA

The lands Genghis Khan first conquered in the 1200s are today the democratic country of Mongolia. Modern Mongolia is located between Russia in the north and the People's Republic of China in the south. The nation's territory stretches 604,830 square miles. That is about the same size as Texas, Oklahoma, New Mexico, and Arizona combined. About 2.7 million people live in Mongolia today. Its capital city is Ulaanbaatar.[22]

countries with a population today of more than 3 billion people.[23] Mongol rule brought safety and peace to those conquered lands. One ancient Persian historian made a surprising claim. He declared that, while the Mongols ruled, a foreign ambassador could travel across Asia with his large official gold seal hanging around his neck and never fear that it would be stolen.[24]

How was it possible for one leader to achieve such a huge success? Temujin started life humbly. After the death of his father, it was uncertain if he would survive at all. But the boy who would become Genghis Khan was strong, smart, and full of ambition. He first became leader of his clan. Then he made it his goal to unite all of the Mongol people into one nation. It took skill and wisdom to fulfill this dream.

"I look upon the nation as a new-born child," Genghis Khan once remarked, "and I care for my soldiers as if they were my brothers."[25] Genghis Khan was a generous man. He was also a man of simple habits. "I wear the same clothing and eat the same food as the cowherds and horseherders," he declared. "We make the same sacrifices, and we share the riches."[26]

Genghis Khan understood the importance of loyalty. He remained loyal to his ally Ong Khan for many years and demanded the same kind of loyalty from his own soldiers. In building his army, he rewarded his troops according to their skills. A soldier's rank depended on his ability, not on noble birth. A lowly shepherd could rise to become the commander of a regiment. These Mongol soldiers were trained to do anything Genghis Khan asked of them. Giovanni de Plano Carpini wrote in 1247 that Genghis Khan "understood how to win over his own countrymen, so that they willingly followed him . . ."[27]

Genghis Khan was a careful leader. He chose the best generals and government officials he could find. Once he had chosen them, he put his trust in them. He thoughtfully organized his army and his empire. His caution helped make him a success.

Genghis Khan also understood that knowledge is power. Throughout his life, he was constantly learning. He gathered scholars and wise men about him and questioned them. When he invaded the Jin Empire, he realized horseback warfare would not capture forts and cities. He quickly adapted and learned how to use siege machines. With siege towers and catapults, he broke down walls and defeated his enemies.

The Persian historian Juvaini would later call Genghis Khan "Courageous, bloody and cruel."[28] It is uncertain how ruthless Genghis Khan truly was. He realized that terror was a valuable military tool. He was glad to have frightening stories told of his soldiers. Many fearful enemies surrendered without putting up a fight. Enemies who resisted the Mongols were treated harshly. In part, they were slaughtered because Genghis Khan did not want to have to fight them again later.

The Mongol steppes were a hard place to grow up. Genghis Khan had learned to live by its violent customs. By comparison, he was less cruel than his anda Jamuka. He was no more cruel than Shah Muhammad and many other leaders of his day, in Asia and in Europe.[29] He was, however, more successful. As a result, more stories are told of his ruthlessness.

Having boldly created an empire, Genghis Khan ruled it brilliantly. Law and order made it possible for his people to thrive. *The Great Yasa,* the *Bilig,* the arrow messenger service, and the use of the Uygur alphabet all brought law, order, and valuable information to the Mongols. Peaceful trade along the Silk Road enriched the empire from one end to the other. Genghis Khan could take deserved pride in the accomplishments of his lifetime. Before his death, he could correctly predict, "A mighty name will remain behind me in the world."[30]

CHRONOLOGY

1162—Temujin is born near the Onon River in Mongolia.

1171—Becomes engaged to Borte of the Onggirat clan; his father is poisoned by Tartars and dies.

ca. 1176—Murders his half-brother Begter; is made a prisoner of the Taijiut clan and escapes.

1178—Marries Borte and forms alliance with Toghrul, leader of the Kereit tribe.

1179—With Toghrul and Jamuka, defeats Merkit tribe; travels with Jamuka's clan for a year and a half.

1189—Declared Genghis Khan, leader of the Mongols, and reorganizes his camp and army.

1196—Raids Tatar territory with Toghrul; Toghrul is named Ong Khan.

1197–1201—Battles various clans in order to strengthen his claim as Mongol leader.

1202—Defeats the Tatar tribe to the east.

1203—Is betrayed by Ong Khan; retreats to Lake Baljuna; makes a surprise attack on the Kereit tribe and defeats them.

1204—Defeats the Naiman tribe and becomes ruler of all the central Asian steppe; adopts Uyghur writing for his people.

1205—Executes his rival and anda brother Jamuka.

1206—Declares the Mongol people a united nation; orders the writing of *The Great Yasa* and the *Bilig*, his laws and his sayings; reorganizes the arrow messenger service.

1207–1210—Makes war upon the Tangut tribe to the southwest.

1211–1214—Makes war upon the Jin Empire to the southeast.

1215—Captures the Jin city of Zhongdu.

1217–1218—Conquers enemies in Kara Khitai to the west.

1219—Declares war against the Khwarizm Empire to the west.

1220—Captures the Khwarizm cities of Bukhara and Samarkand.

1221–1222—Destroys rebellious Khwarizm cities of Herat, Merv, Balkh, Gurganj, Nishapur, and Bamiyan.

1221–1223—Mongol generals Jebei and Subodei raid northwestward as far as the Dnieper River.

1222–1225—Makes long journey back to Mongolia.

1226–1227—At war against rebellious Tanguts; captures the city of Ningxia; dies in August 1227.

1229—His son Ogodei named Great Khan; Ogodei establishes capital at Karakorum.

1236–1242—Mongols, led by grandson Batu, raid into Europe and reach as far as the Danube River.

1251—Grandson Mongke named Great Khan.

1253–1259—Grandson Hulegu conquers territory from Afghanistan to the Mediterranean Sea.

1262—Grandson Kublai named Great Khan; establishes his capital at Zhongdu in China.

1272—Kublai builds new capital called Khanbalik (present-day Beijing).

1275–1292—Italian Marco Polo serves at the court of Kublai Khan.

1300s—Bubonic plague partly responsible for breakup of the Mongol Empire.

CHAPTER NOTES

CHAPTER 2. THE MONGOL BOYHOOD OF TEMUJIN

1. E. D. Phillips, *The Mongols* (New York: Frederick A. Praeger Publishers, 1969), p. 15.

2. Paul Ratchnevsky, *Genghis Khan: His Life and Legacy* (Oxford, United Kingdom: Blackwell Publishers, 1991), p. 7.

3. Christopher P. Atwood, *Encyclopedia of Mongolia and the Mongol Empire* (Indiana University: Facts On File, Inc., 2004), p. 110.

4. Ratchnevsky, p. 12.

5. Ibid.

6. Ibid., p. 8.

7. Leo De Hartog, *Genghis Khan: Conqueror of the World* (New York: Barnes & Noble Books, 1989), p. 8.

8. Ratchnevsky, pp. 16–17.

9. Ibid., p. 17.

10. Michael Prawdin, *The Mongol Empire: Its Rise and Legacy* (London: George Allen and Unwin Ltd., 1961), p. 23.

11. H. Desmond Martin, *The Rise of Chingis Khan and His Conquest of North China* (New York: Octagon Books, 1971), p. 19.

12. Ratchnevsky, p. 145.

13. Arthur Waley, *History of the Mongols* (London: George Allen and Unwin Ltd., 1963), p. 225.

14. Y. A. Vladimirtsov, *The Life of Chingis-Khan* (New York: Benjamin Blom, 1969), p. 17.

15. Ratchnevsky, p. 23.

Chapter 3. The Young Chieftain

1. Paul Ratchnevsky, *Genghis Khan: His Life and Legacy* (Oxford, United Kingdom: Blackwell Publishers, 1991), p. 28.
2. Ibid., pp. 28–29.
3. Ibid., p. 29.
4. Ibid.
5. Peter Brent, *Genghis Khan: The Rise, Authority and Decline of Mongol Power* (New York: McGraw-Hill Book Company, 1976), p. 19.
6. Michael Prawdin, *The Mongol Empire: Its Rise and Legacy* (London: George Allen and Unwin Ltd., 1961), pp. 38–39.
7. Ratchnevsky, p. 35.
8. Arthur Waley, *History of the Mongols* (London: George Allen & Unwin Ltd., 1963), p. 240.
9. Jack Weatherford, *Genghis Khan and the Making of the Modern World* (New York: Crown Publishers, 2004), p. 36.
10. Y. A. Vladimirtsov, *The Life of Chingis-Khan* (New York: Benjamin Blom, 1969), p. 34.

Chapter 4. Khan of the Mongols

1. Paul Ratchnevsky, *Genghis Khan: His Life and Legacy* (Oxford, United Kingdom: Blackwell Publishers, 1991), pp. 40–41.
2. Peter Brent, *Genghis Khan: The Rise, Authority and Decline of Mongol Power* (New York: McGraw-Hill Book Company, 1976), p. 24.
3. The editors of Time-Life Books, *The Mongol Conquests Time Frame AD 1200–1300* (Alexandria, Va.: Time-Life Books, 1989), p. 10.
4. Ratchnevsky, p. 44.

5. Christopher P. Atwood, *Encyclopedia of Mongolia and the Mongol Empire* (Indiana University: Facts On File, Inc., 2004), p. 99.

6. Ratchnevsky, p. 40.

7. H. Desmond Martin, *The Rise of Chingis Khan and His Conquest of North China* (New York: Octagon Books, 1971), pp. 68–69.

8. Atwood, pp. 588–589.

9. Ratchnevsky, pp. 55–56.

10. Ibid., p. 55.

11. Arthur Waley, *History of the Mongols* (London: George Allen & Unwin Ltd, 1963), p. 260.

12. Martin, p. 73.

13. Waley, p. 254.

14. Michael Prawdin, *The Mongol Empire: Its Rise and Legacy* (London: George Allen and Unwin Ltd., 1961), p. 49.

15. Leo De Hartog, *Genghis Khan: Conqueror of the World* (New York: Barnes & Noble Books, 1989), p. 22.

CHAPTER 5. THE CONQUEST OF MONGOLIA

1. Paul Ratchnevsky, *Genghis Khan: His Life and Legacy* (Oxford, United Kingdom: Blackwell Publishers, 1991), p. 68.

2. H. Desmond Martin, *The Rise of Chingis Khan and His Conquest of North China* (New York: Octagon Books, 1971), p. 78.

3. Michael Prawdin, *The Mongol Empire: Its Rise and Legacy* (London: George Allen and Unwin Ltd., 1961), p. 67.

4. Ratchnevsky, p. 81.

5. Ibid., p. 82.

6. Ibid., p. 83.

7. Martin, p. 87.

8. Ibid., p. 88.

9. Y. A. Vladimirtsov, *The Life of Chingis-Khan* (New York: Benjamin Blom, 1969), pp. 60–61.

10. Ibid.

11. Jack Weatherford, *Genghis Khan and the Making of the Modern World* (New York: Crown Publishers, 2004), p. 62.

12. Ratchnevsky, p. 86.

13. Christopher P. Atwood, *Encyclopedia of Mongolia and the Mongol Empire* (Indiana University: Facts On File, Inc., 2004), p. 20.

14. Ratchnevsky, p. 86.

15. Martin, p. 105.

16. Ibid.

Chapter 6. Under the Eternal Blue Sky

1. Jack Weatherford, *Genghis Khan and the Making of the Modern World* (New York: Crown Publishers, 2004), p. 65.

2. Peter Brent, *Genghis Khan: The Rise, Authority and Decline of Mongol Power* (New York: McGraw-Hill Book Company, 1976), p. 42.

3. Paul Ratchnevsky, *Genghis Khan: His Life and Legacy* (Oxford, United Kingdom: Blackwell Publishers, 1991), p. 98.

4. Christopher P. Atwood, *Encyclopedia of Mongolia and the Mongol Empire* (Indiana University: Facts On File, Inc., 2004), p. 489.

5. Ibid., p. 78.

6. H. Desmond Martin, *The Rise of Chingis Khan and His Conquest of North China* (New York: Octagon Books, 1971), p. 96.

7. Ratchnevsky, pp. 90–93.

8. Ibid., p. 93.

9. Martin, p. 23.

10. Ratchnevsky, p. 194.

11. Martin, p. 43.

12. Y. A. Vladimirtsov, *The Life of Chingis-Khan* (New York: Benjamin Blom, 1969), p. 73.

13. Weatherford, p. 72.

14. Michael Prawdin, *The Mongol Empire: Its Rise and Legacy* (London: George Allen and Unwin Ltd., 1961), p. 99.

15. Arthur Waley, *History of the Mongols* (London: George Allen & Unwin Ltd., 1963), p. 290.

16. Weatherford, p. 85.

17. Martin, p. 119.

CHAPTER 7. WAR AGAINST THE JIN EMPIRE

1. Peter Brent, *Genghis Khan: The Rise, Authority and Decline of Mongol Power* (New York: McGraw-Hill Book Company, 1976), p. 52.

2. Paul Ratchnevsky, *Genghis Khan: His Life and Legacy* (Oxford, United Kingdom: Blackwell Publishers, 1991), p. 109.

3. Ibid., p. 108.

4. Jack Weatherford, *Genghis Khan and the Making of the Modern World* (New York: Crown Publishers, 2004), p. 84.

5. Ibid., p. 94.

6. H. Desmond Martin, *The Rise of Chingis Khan and His Conquest of North China* (New York: Octagon Books, 1971), p. 168.

7. E. D. Phillips, *The Mongols* (New York: Frederick A. Praeger Publishers, 1969), p. 56.

8. Michael Prawdin, *The Mongol Empire: Its Rise and Legacy* (London: George Allen and Unwin Ltd., 1961), p. 130.
9. Ratchnevsky, pp. 113–114.
10. Martin, pp. 173–174.
11. Leo De Hartog, *Genghis Khan: Conqueror of the World* (New York: Barnes & Noble Books, 1989), pp. 69–70.
12. Brent, p. 59.
13. Ibid., p. 60.

Chapter 8. Fighting the Khwarizm Empire

1. Paul Ratchnevsky, *Genghis Khan: His Life and Legacy* (Oxford, United Kingdom: Blackwell Publishers, 1991), p. 120.
2. Leo De Hartog, *Genghis Khan: Conqueror of the World* (New York: Barnes & Noble Books, 1989), p. 86.
3. Ratchnevsky, p. 123.
4. E. D. Phillips, *The Mongols* (New York: Frederick A. Praeger Publishers, 1969), p. 60.
5. Jack Weatherford, *Genghis Khan and the Making of the Modern World* (New York: Crown Publishers, 2004), pp. 124–125.
6. Ibid., p. 125.
7. Ibid., p. 5.
8. The editors of Time-Life Books, *The Mongol Conquests Time Frame AD 1200–1300* (Alexandria, Va.: Time-Life Books, 1989), p. 9.
9. Michael Prawdin, *The Mongol Empire: Its Rise and Legacy* (London: George Allen and Unwin Ltd., 1961), p. 169.
10. Weatherford, pp. 111–112.
11. Ibid., p. 113.

150

12. Ibid., p. 114.

13. Tim Severin, *In Search of Genghis Khan* (New York: Atheneum, 1992), p. 169.

14. Ratchnevsky, pp. 131–132.

15. De Hartog, pp. 102–103.

16. Prawdin, p. 212.

17. Weatherford, p. 142.

18. Peter Brent, *Genghis Khan: The Rise, Authority and Decline of Mongol Power* (New York: McGraw-Hill Book Company, 1976), p. 73.

19. Phillips, pp. 62–63.

20. Weatherford, p. 111.

21. Ibid., p. 117.

22. *The Rubaiyat of Omar Khayyam*, translated by Edward Fitzgerald (Greenwich, Conn.: New York Graphic Society, 1966), unpaged.

23. Brent, p. 72.

CHAPTER 9. THE WORLD CONQUEROR

1. The editors of Time-Life Books, *The Mongol Conquests Time Frame AD 1200–1300* (Alexandria, Va.: Time-Life Books, 1989), p. 14.

2. Peter Brent, *Genghis Khan: The Rise, Authority and Decline of Mongol Power* (New York: McGraw-Hill Book Company, 1976), p. 69.

3. H. Desmond Martin, *The Rise of Chingis Khan and His Conquest of North China* (New York: Octagon Books, 1971), p. 2.

4. Michael Prawdin, *The Mongol Empire: Its Rise and Legacy* (London: George Allen and Unwin Ltd., 1961), p. 221.

5. Martin, p. 289.

6. Prawdin, p. 228.

7. Ibid., p. 224.

8. Brent, pp. 77–79.

9. Ibid., p. 79.

CHAPTER 10. MONGOL INVADERS

1. Tim Severin, *In Search of Genghis Khan* (New York: Atheneum, 1992), p. 59.

2. Jack Weatherford, *Genghis Khan and the Making of the Modern World* (New York: Crown Publishers, 2004), p. 146.

3. Ibid., p. 148.

4. Peter Brent, *Genghis Khan: The Rise, Authority and Decline of Mongol Power* (New York: McGraw-Hill Book Company, 1976), p. 118.

5. Weatherford, p. 152.

6. H. Desmond Martin, *The Rise of Chingis Khan and His Conquest of North China* (New York: Octagon Books, 1971), p. 36.

7. Weatherford, p. 155.

8. Paul Ratchnevsky, *Genghis Khan: His Life and Legacy* (Oxford, United Kingdom: Blackwell Publishers, 1991), p. 154.

9. Severin, p. 17.

10. Ibid., 51.

11. Brent, p. 138.

12. Ibid., p. 102.

13. Weatherford, p. 198.

14. Marco Polo, *The Travels* (London: Penguin Books, 1958), pp. 121–122.

15. Ibid., p. 125.

16. Ibid., p. 147.

17. Ibid., p. 156.

18. E. D. Phillips, *The Mongols* (New York: Frederick A. Praeger Publishers, 1969), pp. 106–107.

19. Weatherford, pp. 242–243.

20. Christopher P. Atwood, *Encyclopedia of Mongolia and the Mongol Empire* (Indiana University: Facts On File, Inc., 2004), p. 41.

21. Brent, p. 71.

22. Atwood, pp. 369–370.

23. Weatherford, p. xviii.

24. Leo De Hartog, *Genghis Khan: Conqueror of the World* (New York: Barnes & Noble Books, 1989), p. 144.

25. Ratchnevsky, p. 149.

26. Weatherford, pp. 129–130.

27. Ratchnevsky, pp. 167–168.

28. Brent, p. 107.

29. De Hartog, p. 143.

30. Weatherford, p. 129.

GLOSSARY

ambassador—An official agent or representative.

anda—Blood brother.

bearer—One who carries.

caravan—A group of travelers journeying together through desert or dangerous regions.

curds—Sour milk which thickens into a solid.

engineer—The maker and/or operator of a machine.

evidently—Clearly or obviously.

friar—A member of a religious order.

garrison—The troops stationed at a military post.

khan—Leader.

kumiss—An alcoholic drink made from mare's milk.

kuriltai—A meeting of Mongols, often to choose a new leader.

lance—A steel-tipped spear.

launch—To set in motion or spring forward.

mallet—A long stick with a wooden head on it for striking a ball.

monk—The male member of a religious order who lives in a monastery; friar.

plague—A disease causing much death; epidemic.

porcelain—In pottery and tableware, a clay fired at high temperature and covered with a white glaze.

quiver—A case for carrying or holding arrows.

seal—A device with a raised symbol, emblem, or word used as an official mark of office.

siege—A military blockade of a city or fort in order to force its surrender.

slaughter—To kill great numbers of human beings or animals.

spittle—Saliva; spit.

standardized—Compared with a standard, established, or regular form.

textile—Cloth or fabric.

thicket—A dense growth of bushes or small trees.

tumen—A Mongol army unit consisting of 10,000 men.

twine—A strong string.

yak—A large, longhaired ox found in central Asia.

yurt—A tent-like home made of felt stretched over a wooden frame.

FURTHER READING

Greenblatt, Miriam. *Genghis Khan and the Mongol Empire.* San Diego: Lucent Books, 2001.

Lange, Brenda. *Genghis Khan.* Philadelphia: Chelsea House Publishers, 2003.

Rice, Earl, Jr. *Empire in the East: The Story of Genghis Khan.* Greensboro, N.C.: Morgan Reynolds Publisher, 2005.

Streissguth, Tom. *Genghis Khan's Mongol Empire.* San Diego: Lucent Books, 2005.

Taylor, Robert. *Life in Genghis Khan's Mongolia.* San Diego: Lucent Books, 2000.

Whiting, Jim. *The Life and Times of Genghis Khan.* Newark, Del.: Mitchell Lane Publishers, Inc., 2006.

INTERNET ADDRESSES

THE LOS ANGELES COUNTY MUSEUM OF ART: THE
LEGACY OF GENGHIS KHAN
<http://www.lacma.org/Khan>

NATIONAL GEOGRAPHIC SITE—GENGHIS KHAN
<http://www.nationalgeographic.com/genghis>

ROYAL ALBERTA MUSEUM VIRTUAL EXHIBIT
<http://www.royalalbertamuseum.ca/vexhibit/genghis/
intro.htm>

INDEX